THANK YOU
FOR HEART +L
THAT WE SHARE
NATERALLY. MAY O
PATHS CONTINUE TO
AND PARALLEL THROUGHO
LIVES.

2·11·15

SIX STEPS TO
LIVING ON
PURPOSE

By L. Leonard Taylor

Published By

Lahaina, Hawaii, USA

For my parents, Charles and LeClaire
Taylor, and those before them, whose
shoulders I am privileged to stand upon

"Our deepest fear is not that we are inadequate. Our deepest fear is that we are powerful beyond measure. It is our light, not our darkness that most frightens us. We ask ourselves, Who am I to be brilliant, gorgeous, talented, fabulous? Actually, who are you not to be? You are a child of God. Your playing small does not serve the world. There is nothing enlightened about shrinking so that other people won't feel insecure around you. We are all meant to shine, as children do. We were born to make manifest the glory of God that is within us. It's not just in some of us; it's in everyone. And as we let our own light shine, we unconsciously give other people permission to do the same. As we are liberated from our own fear, our presence automatically liberates others."

~ Marianne Williamson

TABLE OF CONTENTS

Preface

We go through life changing from moment to moment and, over time, become different people according to our environmental conditioning, beliefs and desires. We also change as a result of traumatic and significant events like losing someone close, end of a long term relationship or our own near death experience. Change, by chance, happens whether we like it or not. But what about the times when we consciously want a change? What do we do when we want to rid ourselves of bad habits, dump our frustrating lives or just want out of impossible situations? What if we want to embrace something new, accomplish something different, be something we have never been or have something we have never had?

At some point in our lives, most of us want to change, transform our lives or go beyond previous accomplishments. Obstacles are always in the way or appear as overwhelming challenges. Professionals in the fields of human development have studied endlessly on improving or changing the psychological make up of individuals so we can perform better or differently. From prison to military boot camp, group transformation has been made with success but individual change on demand has proven to be a far greater challenge.

We know that change on demand has been difficult not only because we have been short on knowledge and tools but often we were misdirected, short on commitment and lacked the passion that would move us forward in a new quest. We like our comfort zones and moving outside of them requires strength of purpose, which comes with real hunger and a strong belief in our direction. Without real conviction, we waddle in self created ruts, do the same things over, and over, hoping something will magically deliver us different results.

We know that revamping our lives is possible. History has documented the greatest people known to man, and today we witness the living great ones in the media. We've heard all kinds of inspirational stories of people overcoming terrible odds to become outstanding individuals doing wondrous things. We owe to ourselves and those who have come before us, to be all that we can be and to inspire those who follow us. And, one day we will come to realize that everyone has seeds of greatness and we are all responsible for watering those seeds so that world bears the fruit we all desire!

May the world benefit from you stepping into your transformation.

L. Leonard Taylor

Introduction

I hated my life. My second marriage was ending, my beloved children were with their mothers. I had fallen from grace on my job—I was demoted and demoralized. My income was half of my expenses, I rented my car to a coworker because I could not afford the car payment. I lacked any real friends and my social skills were limited. I was an understated introvert afraid of my own shadow. Yes, I was a shadow of a man. I was financially, emotionally and spiritually bankrupt. At 33 years of age, I was a broken man with a broken life, and I hated it.

Yet somehow I knew I had something greater in me, I knew I had something worthy to give the world. I knew I was better than what I was giving and getting from my less than mediocre life. All around me was the same uninspired life. I wanted more, so much more, but had no clue how to find life beyond my day to day existence, doing the same things over and over. Getting off this merry-go-round seemed impossible.

I made a desperate attempt to find some direction with one of the last purchases of my soon to be cancelled credit card. From a mail order catalogue, I found an audio program - Seeds of Greatness by Dennis Waitley. I knew nothing about this man but the promotion suggested that with this program there was a chance to find a better life. What did I have to lose? Weeks later, the package arrived and I became obsessed with Dr. Waitley's take on life and belief in how much human's can achieve.

Dr. Waitley represented a new beginning. He was offering a ticket on a train I had never traveled. I listened to his words, so many words, of hope and encouragement and did not hesitate to get onboard. This train started moving, with my desire for a better life and to be a better man, I could envision clear rails ahead of me. I began gleaning practical information from my new friend, and the first two steps toward change became very clear.

I surrounded myself with inspirational speakers, agents of change and leaders with new messages of hope. I began soaking in their positive messages, that filled me with unlimited possibilities for a better life. Their messages led me to setting goals for the first time in my life, moving me to re-educate myself and study subjects that would eventually help me find the life I never had but always imagined. I delved into subjects that helped me understand how I had come to my beliefs and other subjects that challenged what I had accepted as truths about myself and my world.

My obsession to change drew me to subjects like mind control, self hypnosis, subconscious programming, subliminal messaging, therapeutic music, all of which I crafted into useful tools and methods to usher in my own transformation. Slowly, without realizing, I began formulating a process that would alter my life forever.

From the gifts of so many others, I created this handbook – a tailored process for change. This book summarizes, in a simple step by step process, how to create and implement a personal program for real and significant change.

"In order to have something you've never had or be something you've never been, you'll have to do something you've never done!"

~ Anonymous

The Process for Effective Change

This process for effective change is not rocket science though every step of this process has brain and mind science at its core. The simple steps here have been derived from numerous sources and combined to create a program requiring minimal time, painless effort and little money. Aspects of this process could be viewed as techniques used in brainwashing. "Brainwashing" is most often associated with secret cults, murderous madmen or even government programming while the word itself, could be compared with something as useful as bathing, doing laundry or washing a car. Considering the negative connotations "brainwashing" conjures up for us, lets refer to this part of the process as it is "brain cleansing."

I believe it is our responsibility to cleanse our brains regularly, for the same reason we clean anything. We absolutely need to flush out the uselessly old, habitually bad and the fictitiously false thoughts and beliefs we pick up on our way to wherever we are headed. There is no wonder why we too often continue down the same path hoping for different results—we never seem to voluntarily clean our brains with updated directions.

With this brain cleanse, we can expect our path to be clear, our focus to be sharpened and our purpose always in the forefront. A good brain cleanse is the simple, very effective and direct method to change the oil, tune up the car, check the tires and wash the car in preparation for a road trip.

However, and more accurately, this process for change involves more than brain-cleansing. It involves the reprogramming and protection of your newly created direction. When followed, you will end up with a program that will take you where you decide to go. Of course, your destination is a choice, so, there must be clarity as to where you are going, who you will be and what you will do. For this reason, a chapter has been included on *How to Find Your Purpose* though the intent of this book is not to define your purpose but to put you on a path of *living* your purpose.

The mission of this book is to offer a process that can be customized individually, to make a major change in your life. There is no real mystery to this process, the power is in the combined use of the individual steps. The individual steps in this book are not new but have been the subject of study by scholars and science,

contemplated by spiritual masters, tested and documented. The six simple steps are plainly identified as:

1) **Stop** or minimize the negative influences in life
(can't see the forest when surrounded by trees.)

2) **Start** adding attitude altering content to daily life
(choose mind food wisely, we are what we eat!)

3) **Assess** current position in this world today (need to
know where you are to plot a destination!)

4) **Plan** life with goals & milestones with a roadmap
(driving cross country is easier with a map!)

5) **Program** the conscious & subconscious with the
same plan (make right & left hands work together!)

6) **Affirm** desires, cement beliefs and ˌreject the
negative (remember to go towards the light).

Individually, these steps are simple to implement.
Together, these steps are powerful life changing tools
giving back personal responsibility, defining direction
and exercising the greatest amount of control over
individual peace and prosperity. This is a simple step by
step "how to" book, using real tools that will result in
significant change. These six steps will deliver
transformation to those seeking major change.

"How long? How long will this take?" is the most frequently asked question. The truthful answer is, the commitment and effort given to the program is directly related to the time required to make a change. If television is discontinued or replaced with a regular diet of positive material, noticeable changes will be observed quickly. An honest assessment and the creation of a solid plan with goals will produce immediate progress. However, a part-time 'off and on' effort could result in failure altogether. Unfortunately, it would be irresponsible to quote the time required in this process for making *your* personal effective change, as it is directly related to your dedication and desire.

For nine months I spent hours researching, experimenting, planning and programming which resulted in success never imagined. Unlike my unplanned approach of identifying programs and building processes, you have the opportunity to immerse yourself from the start. There is no need to take months studying and building a program. You can immediately jump into these six steps and note changes in days and radical transformation in weeks; you are the beneficiary of my exercise and success. I believe you will implement change at a much faster rate. However, caution should be used not to fall into the western expectation of *instant gratification* or discouragement may be the reward.

These steps are simple, but passion and commitment play a significant role in changing long held beliefs, old habits and years of reinforcing programming. Dedicate yourself to this process and create the desirable change in your life painlessly and quickly.

These tools and instructions will lead you through custom designing a program to put you on a track to meet your most ambitious desires. In a simple step by step process, you will learn how to create the change you want in your life.

May your metamorphosis begin now, so that you live the life you desire and your transformation benefits all humanity.

"The mind is much like a computer –
garbage in, garbage out!"
~ Modern American Proverb

Step One:
Stop the Negative Influences in Your Life

Researchers and media experts report that we are bombarded with thousands of negative messages daily. In the first step of this program we will minimize most of these messages from our mainstream media. Adherence to this simple step will significantly impact how fast change can occur. Our mainstream media is filled with negative messages, subliminal messaging and time killing content, all of which are distractions to reaching any destination. With the many things we desire in our lives, we must wrestle away our time from external sources to better direct our attention and energy.

More people complain today about their inability to stay focused on a given task. Most of us have experienced starting a task and a few minutes later find ourselves working on something entirely different. What is at the core of this attention deficit disorder? Well, it is possible that this familiar re-prioritizing of tasks is due to the clutter of an overloaded mind. Today, we are overburdened with tasks and incoming information, in the workplace and at home, which is enough to easily drive us away from our intent to the point of distraction.

You can begin gaining greater control of your life by exercising as much power over external influences as possible. Only you can fully manage the distraction from television, the Internet, radio, music, newspapers, magazines and other media. Uncontrollable audio, visuals and other sources of influence, will be the focus in step six. For now, we will simply eliminate the potential influence of controllable mainstream sources.

The emotional content of television programs can affect your psychological health by directly eliciting positive or negative feelings with particular content. With this kind of mind control, anyone can be shaped and molded into feelings undesired by you but valuable to another. Repeated viewing of television can sell you fear, racial stereotypes or even a lifestyle. Television as debated by psychoologists, also promotes violence, antisocial behavior and affects eating habits among other questionable habits. How it affects you could be a study of its own but there are two things certain, when you stop watching television: you will feel better and you will have more time to dedicate to your purpose or other tasks at hand.

There is no in-between with television. It simply must be turned off during your brain-cleansing. If you watch TV during this time you are limiting your growth and can fail in your attempt to make major change. Do not turn it on, leave it off. While staying away from television can be difficult with others in the same household, this may be a good opportunity to review and rethink what others are watching these days. If the TV is on, even if you are not watching, the blather is still being taken in unconsciously.

Music is best turned off for the duration of your program. If you are an audiophile and must listen to music, there are a few things that you can do to minimize the potential negative effects of music. First, listen to music without vocals. Vocals contain messages, good and bad. We need not try to analyze all of the lyrics to determine what is what, so eliminate vocals all together. Second, listen to new music, music you have not heard. Music, of which you are familiar, has memories and emotions associated to them (conscious and subconscious) that we are purposely trying to quiet during your change program. Third, listen to music from the "baroque" period in history that included major composers Vivaldi, Bach, Handel whose music is now associated with putting the mind into a relaxed beta state where relaxation and learning come with greater ease.

The radio has more than the random uncontrollable selection of music and lyrics that are played, it also has negative content included in news, commercials and jabber. For control purposes, leave it turned off.

Reading materials including random books, popular magazines and regular newspapers are filled with negative, disparaging and even positive seeming materials that can affect self esteem or sell you on a lifestyle that may only be in seller's best interest. Millions of dollars are spent to plant messages in periodicals, that can be taken in with a mere glance. Newspaper writing has become sport with misinformation and an abundance of negative messaging that are legally allowed. Cut your regular monitoring of these sources of information and you will immediately experience greater clarity. Big readers need not worry, in the next step, there are references to some very positive reading materials.

The biggest challenge for most of us today is the Internet which is competing with television as the dominant media source. Like television, we turn on the computer and one thing leads us to another, then another and yet another until we have spent hours downloading and uploading, playing on our favorite social network and forwarding senseless emails. While the Internet has increased productivity in the workplace, it has also become a killer of personal productive time not to mention the effect it has on face to face communications, and its passive mood changing ability.

Today, the Internet is quite often in the palm of our hand which has caused auto accidents, poor vision, rude behavior and most importantly, distraction from our life's purposes. Smartphones are currently the best way to keep us connected when we control our usage and remain present in our real world situations. When we unconsciously lose sight of real world activity while engrossed in our smartphones, we subtly pay a little with our own life and purpose. The real value of smartphones is limited but the value of the life in front of us is priceless.

I gave up my smartphone and tablet during my last brain cleanse, when I realized how addicted I had become. Now, I shake my head when watching other people ignore their friends and children, multitask while driving and miss the life in front of them while ruining their eyes by gluing them to a screen. Here's a big secret to improving your quality of life—turn them off just like the other media sources during your change program. When you complete your program, you'll be very conscious of your smartphone use and wiser in your control. Hey, if you need access, use it, but if you are facebooking and texting friends all day long you might want to try disconnecting, cold turkey, during your transformation program.

When you need to access the computer, smartphone or tablet, write down or consider the specific reasons for access before launching into the device. Try it. It is tough but it can be done. For example, when considering sitting at your computer, make a list and stick to it:

1) Make plane reservations.
2) Send grandma my itinerary.
3) E-mail boss my vacation dates.
4) Book car rental. Done.

Now, with your list in hand, go on-line and do what you intended in one sitting. Unless your on-line social network is part of your business, do you have to access the most addictive activity on the Internet? If you are not on a socializing mission as part of this transition, let go of the extracurricular online socializing. Simply, make a plan and stick to the plan. When you are done with your planned activities, get off, shut down, step back into present reality.

The most uncontrollable sources of influence in our lives are people. We can't control the words coming from the mouths of others. So, until we get to step six, try to limit your exposure to those who constantly spew negativity. In the final step in this process, we will cover some very effective ways to counter the undesired influences of others. For now, forgive them, for they know not what they do.

"You can change who you are, you can change what you are by changing what you put into your mind."

~ Zig Zigler

Step Two:
Start Adding Positive Content to Your Life

Understanding your brain is much like a computer - you can only get out of it a manipulated version of what you put into the machine. If you put in garbage it gets all mixed in and spits out garbage. In step one, we began shutting down the flow of negative, thoughtless, unwanted garbage. In this step, the focus will be on feeding the mind very positive, compelling, motivating and thought provoking possibilities about life. By cutting off the negative and introducing the positive, we begin unlocking any self imposed limitations towards life, through the regular flow of supportive materials.

To begin programming for positive change, your audio player will become your best friend. You will not want to be without your audio player once you begin your new diet of eye awakening messages. I remember getting my first motivational audio program. I immersed myself into Dr. Denis Waitley's *Seeds of Greatness* after listening to a few convincing minutes. Dr. Waitley is not the typical inspirational speaker, he is a PhD in psychology, a former psychology coach for the USA Olympic track team and has counseled diverse groups from world leaders to returning Vietnam prisoners of war. Dr. Waitley is an expert in the field of performance and his 10 secrets started me on my path to new heights of achievement and life has not been the same since.

One memorable moment, while listening to Dr. Waitley's program occurred when I was working on a man's car who was paying me top dollar to install some custom electronics. This was side work to supplement my income and I needed every nickel. I was curious about this car owner who had everything, at such a young age—a beautiful intact family, a huge high end home and fine cars. Unexpectedly, Dan came into his garage at the worst possible time—I had his BMW torn apart with seats, carpet and parts lying all over the place while his Blaupunkt stereo played my motivational program. I saw the disturbed look on his face as I was sure there was going to be a problem. Of course, at this point in my life I expected something negative from Dan because that was what I always expected in my world - problems.

Dan, noticed the mess but was more interested in what I was listening to at that moment. "Hey, who is this guy? Motivational speaker?" A smile was riding across his face now, as Dan had seemingly forgotten his disassembled luxury car. I talked about Waitley, Dan told me about how inspirational speakers helped him on his job. I was relieved there was no drama until he began again.

"You know I have some motivational CDs, you think we could trade?" Was he kidding? Give up my new life blood? Of course, I had listened to this program innumerable times by then but no one could divulge the lessons Denis Waitley bestowed on me. There was no way I was going to part with my new best friend Denis. I delayed, not wanting to disappoint the man who could give me a fat tip. Dan sensed my stress. "Hey, if you don't like the CDs we'll just trade back." I thought this might not be so bad after all.

No sooner than I left Dan's house, with a bigger tip than expected, I put on what sounded like southern Baptist preacher and was immediately disappointed. This wannabe preacher would never get close to Waitley who was bringing me out of darkness. Now, I would have to suffer without my program at least long enough for Dan to hear the Waitley program. I took twenty minutes driving home listening to the preacher and another hour and a half glued to my car seat in my parking lot—I didn't want to turn him off. Zig Zigler, in his wonderful wisdom, weaved point by point, story after story, on how to get what you want and captured my attention. I never looked back.

If motivational or inspirational speaking is new to you, I suggest *Seeds of Greatness*, by Denis Waitley, *How to Get What You Want* by Zig Zigler or *Step Into Your Greatness* by Les Brown to get started. All of these positive programs promote moving you from where you are today in a direction you'd like to go. Denis Waitley speaks of ten secrets to greatness with scientific certainty. Zig Zigler's style of speaking comes from his Mississippi roots, enthusiasm from selling most of his life and heart felt thoughts of how life works. From Les

Brown's humble beginnings, he magically conceived the idea that we all have gifts and greatness to offer the world. He can inspire anyone who may think they are in a hopeless situation. I strongly recommend these speakers that are known for the quality and quantity of their positive messages and ability to keep your attention—you will not be bored.

There's an abundance of inspiring speakers available to you today. I suggest you find other motivational speakers that appeal to you, remain positive through their programs and who never get boring. An important criteria in selecting speakers is to avoid anyone that bases a doctrine on fear and embrace those that encourage growth and build self confidence. Once you have had a good introduction to these kinds of programs, you will easily distinguish what works for you. Until then, I hope you find my recommendations beneficial. However, I do not recommend using material from your past that might have other meanings associated with them, find something new and fresh.

Listen to audio programs whenever possible and often. Repetition is most important and key in changing useless and even detrimental beliefs. The ideas provided in these types of motivational audio programs will sink in with repeated listening. If you are on the road with family or friends, you may want to introduce them to some inspirational listening. Most people find it hard to trivialize positive messages but if you suspect someone will, it might not be worth the negative feedback. Years after exposing family members to my favorite speakers, they still repeat meaningful sound bites and messages picked up from them. You never know who just might like Zig Zigler.

There are a couple of video programs that will help to expand your consciousness without drugs. *The Secret* explains the law of attraction or how the power of our thoughts can deliver exactly what we are thinking. *What the Bleep* describes how the universe may work from a quantum physics basis. Both are theoretical possibilities of life that inspire hope for our ability to personally create beyond what we have assumed up to this point. From a strictly entertaining point of view try the movie, *Limitless*. Believe what you will, but these videos will challenge your sense of all things. They can be bought or rented from your local video store and on-line (when you are on an Internet mission). Also check with your local library for a free check out. In the "Recommendations" of this book, find motivational videos and links to videos.

For reading material, please look at Stephen Covey's *Seven Habits of Highly Successful People* and *The Four Agreements* by Don Miguel Ruiz. These are excellent books that have changed the lives of countless people. Before getting to step four, in this book, please read from Covey's book, the chapter on goal setting—*Begin with the end in mind*. Pay close attention to this chapter in preparation for writing goals. There are audio versions of both books which is an easy way to gobble up the material.

Again, if money is an issue to getting these programs, try your local library first before buying them inexpensively from Amazon, eBay or even Craigslist. No money? Borrow the money, get an advance from your job—do what is necessary to invest in your personal change. If you are committed to making a change, you will find a way to fill your time with positive motivational and inspirational material. Okay, so you do not want to resort to begging? Try this: search Google and youtube.com and you will find hours of great free material. Again, I caution you of the challenge the Internet represents, so, make a plan, get on, get what you need and get off the Internet. Bookmark those good locations to avoid wasting time when hungry for good brain food. Used in the right way, change will occur as you plan!

Lastly, you may find, within recommended programs, references to the speaker's personal beliefs of one kind or another. None of the recommendations I make here are associated with any particular belief system and should you find any material inappropriate for your personal use, then move on to other material though these speakers do not make long points of their personal beliefs. The idea at this point, is to listen to positive, inspirational material that will uplift and offer hope and new possibilities. So, lets get started–get at least one positive program today. See the "Recommendations" in the back of this book for suggestions.

In this life, if we do not pursue what we love, if we do not summon our pain for good or use the best of our knowledge, experience or natural ability, then we may squander a lifetime of gifts, opportunity most beneficial to ourselves, those close to us and all humanity.

One of the motivations for writing this book came after friends visited me in Hawaii with their two teenaged sons. The eldest son, Brian, a senior in high school, was brilliant and had the aptitude to successfully pursue whatever he wanted in life and was at a decision point. The father and mother, both practical people, an engineer and a school teacher, wanted my assistance in pushing Brian into their way of thinking about careers. They respected my opinion having already seen my kids through college, I would surely have their same practical opinion.

My friends came from backgrounds and a time where financial stability was the primary goal and priority in life. They evaluated every opportunity from a financial standpoint and attributed their financial success to the husband's choice of an engineering career, though it may not have been his passion in life. They'd come far from their modest roots and wanted their children to follow proven path.

However, Brian had aspirations and a passion for creating art. He had made inroads at the high school level and a demonstrated capability. He was certain of his ability to prosper as an artist. The parent's legitimate concerns were with the financial uncertainty and lack of security in the art profession, it was just too risky. Brian's points were simple, his personal desire being most important on this subject. After all the points were made a couple times, everyone looked at me, as if I were the tie breaker. "What do you think he should study?" the parents finally asked.

"Well, I don't think there is much of a choice," I paused as the parents beamed their happiness of arriving to what was surely the obvious conclusion. "If there were some way to study both curriculums, I would support such an effort. But if there is only one choice between being safe or being passionate about life, well, I think of it like this: What would become of Brian's spirit if he studied engineering and never studied art? What would happen to his

passion for life and art? I think Brian should follow his passion if it isn't based on his ego. If earning a living or doing something that is financially safe are the only criteria for choosing an occupation, then engineering is the way to go."

Brian was elated. The parents, wholly regretful for asking my opinion, have not spoken to me since ₁then. I have no doubt that we should consider the priority of passion as an element in our own happiness. However, passion is not the sole factor.

How to Find Your Purpose

Knowing your purpose is the beginning of every journey. In this chapter, you will identify your reason for being here and how you may best affect humanity. To find your purpose is to identify the life that can deliver the greatest satisfaction, personal peace, rewarding prosperity and best service to others. You will also gain an understanding of the biggest obstacles to your living your purpose with integrity.

To know your purpose is to be consciously aware of what you can do in this life to positively affect humanity. However, this is just the beginning in preparation to put you on the path of living your purpose with virtuous principles. This process is an effective tool, guiding you to identifying your personal purpose in life. Only after you have identified your personal purpose will you be ready to begin the third step of *Six Steps to Living On Purpose*.

To live your purpose is to identify the path chosen as your personal destiny and not one of the essential steps in this book. The six step method of change found here is not dependent on any particular goal but a well defined goal and solid purpose. This book will, indeed catapult your purpose in the direction of your desires. *Six Steps to Living On Purpose* will put you on a pathway to reach your goals, be they noble or treacherous. However, it would be irresponsible to demonstrate such a life changing, humanity impacting, powerful tool without consideration of those who might pursue a purpose that would negatively impact the world. If you already have a purpose or do not wish to consider your life's effect on humanity, the statement of warning below was written specifically for you.

Warning: Using the six step transformational process requires a well defined thought-through purpose, preferably a "Life Purpose." Implementation of something other than your clear life purpose may lead to greed and excessive ego resulting in unhappiness, feelings of an unfulfilled life and have a negative impact on humanity. Please read this chapter "How to Find Your Purpose" to clearly identify your life's purpose before continuing.

The Philosophy of Purpose

Purpose, is our reason for being here, the justification for our existence, the thing we are meant to do in this life. Our purpose for living has been and will be the topic of philosophical discussions for ages to come. This chapter does not expect to answer the question but to lay the foundation from which this process is based, in search of your personal purpose.

In our changing world, it has become apparent that our survival as a species is dependent on our ability to work together as a species or, alternatively, continue down the path of self annihilation (extinction). Understanding that the former is the choice of most, there is a need to find common ground in order to meet the challenges of climate change, overpopulation, depletion of earth resources and to simply meet the needs of all people.

Perpetuating the species of man is in line with the natural order of all life - plant and animal. The dominant world religions, maintain the belief that man's purpose here is to "glorify God". Glorifying God may be interpreted in many ways though maintaining God's creation - people, planet and all life - would be universally accepted by religions. Maintaining life on earth, as a primary purpose of mankind, aligns with other dominant groups based in science or secular philosophies. This process for finding your purpose is based on the dominantly held belief that _we are here to serve each other or serve life itself_, the same life and balance in nature that supports mankind.

Believing that serving life is man's purpose for living, there must be some agreement as to what measures are required or what driving principles all men can agree to that will be a binding belief that all others may be judged. Where there are principles, there is always room for descent and anything that binds humankind will have to stand up to constant scrutiny. Are there principles that can be agreed upon by all humankind? Yes, there are at least two of which that people and not necessarily governments, can agree.

First and foremost, every person should be allowed and have the right to prosper. That is, every person should have the opportunity to seek and maintain plenty of what they need to survive. Specifically, all physiological needs such as food, water, shelter, safety, reproduction, rest, and livable environment. To have plenty of what you need, by definition, is *prosperity*.

The second principle of purpose, that man can agree upon, is everyone's right to seek and maintain their desired life without disturbance. Disturbance, in this case, is defined as the interruption of a settled or peaceful condition. Everyone agrees in their right to seek and maintain there own *peace.*

Adding to the foundation of man's purpose - *to serve life* - are the two principles of purpose - Prosperity and Peace. These same principles can also be applied to man's environment by allowing nature to prosper without disturbance within the bounds of allowing man to survive. With these agreements we can proceed with finding personal purposes.

"When you are inspired by some great purpose, some extraordinary project, all your thoughts break their bonds: Your mind transcends limitations, your consciousness expands in every direction, and you find yourself in a new, great and wonderful world. Dormant forces, faculties and talents become alive, and you discover yourself to be a greater person by far than you ever dreamed yourself to be."

~ Patanjali

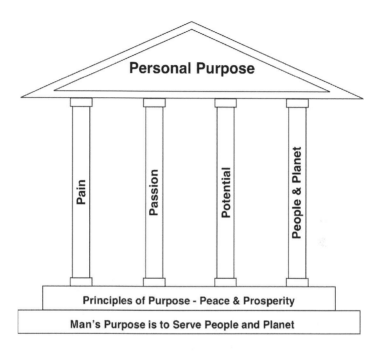

Introduction to the Process of Finding Purpose

Whether you've read the material before this section or not, you can begin the process of identifying personal purpose. The process of finding your personal purpose, your life's purpose, is rather simple and just involves your dedicated time to complete.

The structure of purpose begins with the foundation or mankind's purpose for existing - service to life. The principles of this purpose and the goals of humans are universal - to ensure all are entitled and have rights to seek out and maintain peace and prosperity. By definition personal purpose is aligned with the foundation of humankind's purpose.

This method to finding your purpose begins with four elements of life that are related to the celebrated archetypes of man found in the writings of Carl Jung, Robert Bly and Robert Moore. David Fabricius seizes these concepts in his teachings as key elements to purpose, as well. Your meaningful purpose will consider your enduring pain, current passion, your natural potential and their relationship to other people.

Each of these four areas of our lives are powerful though limited in providing a complete picture of personal purpose on their own. Pain consumes so much of our time that we become experts on this uncomfortable distraction. Passion, often held as our purpose alone, which sometimes changes, can easily take us down a path not in tune with your natural abilities. Potential, our natural, learned skills and experience, can lack motive. While empathy for people may not possess the inspiration to drive a purpose.

During this process, you will brainstorm, shuffle, and define aspects of your life most meaningful to you. You will get naked with yourself, and search out your deepest pains, desires, natural gifts, and empathetic feelings for others. These things become your clues and as you relate the four categories to each other. Your toolbox for living will emerge easily, areas for leadership highlighted, missions of service of which you are well suited become obvious, your gifts to others visibly clear, where you can find your greatest peace and prosperity lay before you. Then, your purpose begins to take shape with meaning that resonates with your life and all will become vividly clear.

The Four Pillars of Purpose
Pain

The pillar of pain is at the heart of personal purpose, as it is usually our central focus and has the greatest impact on our lives. Our minds are consumed with past and possible future events, that are themselves the reasons for our suffering and discomforts. These pains are the result of mental, physical, or emotional trauma that causes us to change our beliefs to protect us from further injury.

Our traumas from childhood, before we developed coping or critical thinking skills, frequently become the stories on which our beliefs are based and have great influence thereafter. Even as adults, unaddressed traumas lead to unwanted beliefs and behaviors. From wherever this pain is derived, it continues to come up at times when we are reminded of the experience. Common trauma from which we suffer include:

- sexual, emotional, and physical abuse
- sustained discrimination
- abject poverty
- terrorism and war
- disasters
- neglect
- medical

We may believe the effects of trauma have been healed, the perpetrators forgiven, and not associate the trailing discomfort and pain with any particular trauma. However, subconscious memory of trauma can be stimulated by visuals, sounds, words and even by a touch, smell or taste. We may be conscious of lasting pain from past trauma, however, left unaddressed, we may not recognize the created beliefs and adapted behavior that have formed.

Our responses to pain or trauma will typically fall into one of three broad categories:

1) negative response: the pain from trauma can result in wildly dangerous beliefs that may lend themselves to feeling separated from others, producing negative and even dangerous behavior;

2) neutral control: aware of pain, we may control our reactions to stimuli although the pain remains;

3) positively addressed: when we positively address our pain, we can move beyond our created beliefs and their auto responses. Addressing pain allows us to heal, change, create new beliefs, help others with similar challenges and be of service to humanity in the elimination of collective pain.

For example, using "sustained discrimination" of African Americans in the USA as an example for each you could find the following results. A negative response to an overwhelming sense of discrimination might result in hatred of those associated with perpetuating the condition, unfairly reacting to all whites in a hostile manner in a perceived discriminatory incident. A neutral response to an overwhelming sense of discrimination, being aware that not all whites discriminate, might be to silently endure the feeling of pain during a perceived discrimination incident. Positively addressing one's pain might be to approach the situation without preconceived ideas of what is taking place, check out the situation properly without attachment and seek justice for all involved.

What are your greatest pains in life? What things seem to trigger undesired behavior for you? Without needing to understand the cause, what ongoing discomforts or pain do you feel in unplanned moments? What causes the pain that has you spend so much time avoiding, contemplating or otherwise focused on, in some way?

If you do not have a major source of recurring pain, discomfort, regrets or hyper sensitivities, ask friends and family or even a mental health professional to be sure you are not suppressing unapproachable pain.

More frequently today, pain, regrets or lasting challenges simply aren't there. The younger you are, the more likely any negative effects of trauma has resulted in lasting pain. Indeed, there are parents and children who have been able to manage or avoid traumatic events without lasting effects. If you are such an individual, you have the promise to epitomize a peaceful existence, effortlessly lead by example and mentor missions of service.

If you are truly pain, discomfort and regret free, then use your deepest empathetic feelings towards the needs of other people or the planet as your healthy approach towards finding purpose. Give in to fervently following your passions and maximizing your potential, which will serve as natural examples to others. What is the source of your most empathetic feelings today? What moves or challenges you regarding the needs and pains of people or planet? What is your greatest empathy for the planet or others?

Don't run away from grief, O soul.
Look for the remedy inside the pain,
Because the rose came from the thorn,
And the ruby from the stone.

~ *Rumi*

Passion

The second pillar of purpose, passion, represents those things that we are just plain psyched out about doing. Passion arouses our enthusiasm, gives us an intense desire to follow or do something. Maybe it's painting, writing, software engineering, swimming, teaching, gardening, cleaning, acting or caring for the challenged. Passion is anything we do that allows time to fly by without realizing, Passion is the willingness to do something without pay when others get paid to do such work. Passion is the element in purpose associated with great fervor, zeal, spirit and abundant energy. Passion supplies the driving energy of our purposes. Passions can change over a lifetime, often after a life changing event. What do you have a great passion for today?

"Passion is energy. Feel the power that comes from focusing on what excites you."

~ Oprah Winfrey

Potential

The third pillar of purpose - potential - is the collection of personal traits, qualities, and natural abilities as recognized by ourselves and others. Natural abilities are often thought of as God given or inherited gifts. They are the attributes that others see in us as natural capabilities to sing, work with numbers, influence people, tell jokes, write, grow plants, critically think, or whatever we might do that stands out as a strength. If we cannot readily identify our natural strengths, we can ask those who knows us well, from parents and friends to teachers and mentors. Gifts can also be those skills we have learned and mastered. Our potential can be taken for granted and therefore not used in ways most beneficial to ourselves or others to advance our purposes in life. What are our natural gifts, skills and abilities?

"All things will be produced in superior quantity and quality, and with greater ease, when each man works at a single occupation, in accordance with his natural gifts, and at the right moment, without meddling with anything else."

~ Plato

People & Planet

The last pillar of purpose - people & planet - is what we bring in service to other people or our life sustaining planet. Ideally, our purpose will be in complete alignment with service to humanity towards peace and prosperity. This pillar of purpose keeps our efforts focused on meeting the needs of all people ensuring all have an opportunity to prosper and have peace.

Secondarily, this pillar of purpose is to predict and measure our progress in serving the needs of life. This is a challenge because it requires self-governance in addition to collective support and feedback. Working as community lifts the entire collective, while reaching our own level of prosperity is required to feel empowered to help another. Our personal pursuits in life can have a negative impact on humanity and only through constant personal consciousness can we monitor the impact we are having on serving life and not separating.

What needs or desires, of <u>people and planet,</u> can we best serve that would also allow us to positively address our <u>pain,</u> that will be energized by our <u>passions</u> and makes use of our full <u>potential</u>? What personal purpose do we believe will make a difference in people and our planet?

The Process of Finding Your Purpose
The pillars of purpose will begin coming to life now as your own specifics are added in the process. The following step by step process is followed with detailed directions and examples. I recommend reading through to the end of the chapter then returning to start and complete the process.

1) Brainstorm and make lists of items, thoughts, ideas, attributes for each pillar (Example on page 53);
2) Combine brainstormed contents, where possible, into common elements under each pillar. You want to end up with one item for pain and people and no more than 2-4 for passions and potential;
3) Pair up and relate each pillar with every other for keys & clues on purpose (see diagram on page 60);
4) Imagine the power of combined keys, clues, and feel your vision of purpose;
5) Write and refine a statement of purpose. Constant review and revision will prove to create a truly representative and believable statement of you;
6) Speak your statement of purpose everyday, several times a day until it is memorized and you own it!

Brainstorming

Pain	_Passion_
People & _Planet_	_Potential_

Take a sheet of paper, divide the sheet into four sections by drawing a big plus sign through the middle and then write the name of each pillar as shown. Read the pillar descriptions below, and begin to brainstorm. Alternatively, there are lots of blank pages in the back of the book for your convenience. When you brainstorm, simply write a few words for each thought or idea that comes to mind without judging or thinking about them in the moment. Write these in the corresponding quadrant. Later you will work with these items to pinpoint the most fitting and worthy subjects in each category.

This work is personal and need not be shared with anyone, however, it is important to be honest with yourself. Your pain may be challenging to confront or admit. Your passions could be embarrassing to expose to others. You may think of your potential as meaningless or arrogant in the face of others. What you believe beneficial to people may not appear so useful to you, but there is a place in this world for every gift to meet a real need or desire. Take your time so as not to miss the big or little items, you'll sort them out later. Use the questions below to prompt your brainstorming in each quadrant.

Pain - What hurts when you think about it? What kind of situations, conversations or movies do you avoid? What do you do that negatively impacts your life or the lives of others? What creates fear, discomfort, changes in your moods or behavior? What stops you from doing certain things? What triggers quick changes in behavior? Try to pin down one or more things that come to mind. If you have nothing to list, substitute pain with empathy. What strongly held empathy do you have for others?

Passion - What is something do you just love to do? If you had everything in life you needed, what would you do? What gives you energy, arouses lasting enthusiasm, and allows you to get lost while you are doing it? What would you do for free that others get paid to do today? List at least one passion that qualifies as something you love, would do for free, and you could get lost in doing.

Potential - What are you naturally good at doing? What things do you do better than many or most others? What are you recognized for by others? What have parents, guardians, friends and teachers recognized in you as extraordinary? What skills and abilities have you learned that you are now exceptional at using? List these things as your natural gifts or learned skills and abilities that standout.

People & Planet - When you look at the world and see challenges and needs of people, plants, animals and earth, what do you find to be of great need. What need or desire of others do you feel you would be good at meeting? What cause or challenge do you feel called to contribute time, energy, or money? What cause, challenge, need or desire, do you feel you could be of great assistance? List those things that could make a difference in the lives of others, be they needs or desires.

Combining and Tightening Contents
Now, if at all possible, we want to narrow the contents of this brainstorm down to one cohesive meaningful representation for each category. Here we want to

combine items with a common theme and eliminate any items that aren't strongly felt.

Below are the results of my brainstorm as an example:

Pains	Passions
Prejudice & Discrimination	Writing
Social & Nature Injustices	Video & Photography
Heartbreak from Love	Mysteries, History & Truth
Snobbery & Rejection	Inspirational Stories
People & Planet	**Potential**
Opportunity to Prosper	Translating Between Groups
Accountable Leadership	Communicating/ Marketing
Justice & Peace	Organizing & Team Build
How to Get on Track	Creative Problem Solving

The following are example statements created from my above brainstormed list after being combined and tightened.

<u>Pain</u> - There is a common thread between three of the four items listed under the pain pillar with *Heartbreak from Love* being the odd one. I combine *Prejudices & Discrimination, Social & Nature Injustices and Snobbery & Rejection* to become something that resonates with me. The painful feeling of being unfairly judged, discriminated against or rejected boils down to feeling separated from others, which appears to be a common theme. Experiencing any one of these three items results in that same painful feeling. However, the *Heartbreak from Love* and stands alone from the other theme.

In comparison, the heartbreak is not nearly as strong and definitely secondary in the big scheme of pain. Because of the strong feelings in the one area of life, I will focus my attention on the three dominant indicators of pain I experience. I am not letting go of this secondary source of pain, it too needs to be dealt with but one pain at a time for now. Summarizing this life affecting pain, I've come to this statement: *My pain is feeling less than others and believing that I am not as significant to mankind, as others.*

Take your time with the items identified as painful and combine those that are similar, eliminate those that are not truly critical or are secondary in nature. Find a common theme if more than one item remains. Write a simple statement of your pain. If you have no pain, then write a statement of your most empathetic feeling of the pain of other people or the planet.

Passion - I have a lot of passions, this could be tricky. However, when I begin considering what I like about each of these items, I realize there is a common theme. In general and common to all passions here, are stories - creating stories via writing, video & photography as much as reading, listening to and watching stories. Knowledge of self quickly gives me that understanding, without any doubt. I may not consciously know how these things will play solidly into my purpose, at this point but *My passion is storytelling.*

Passions are not whims or things you might like, so first eliminate those items of which you are not certain. If you have more than one item remaining, find the common theme. If you have no passions, identify one thing you would really like to try, sample, or give a chance. Write a simple statement for your passion.

Potential - These items don't appear very related in any way but when I stop to consider what could be done with these skills and abilities, I can envision alignment with man's greater purpose to serve each other. I can see a bigger picture of bringing people together, solving problems between them, organizing using my communications and marketing skills to find common ground. Wow, this is something I would not have considered. I might want someone objective, who knows me, to tell me what they think of this. On the other hand, my heart is beating as if I know I am being called to do something now. *My potential, natural and learned gifts, is in bringing people and projects together for execution.*

Potential are gifts that you possess, that you may or may not use. If you are not using these gifts, ask yourself if they are truly gifts and eliminate those that are not exceptional and look for a common connection between the remaining gifts. Write a simple statement of your natural and learned skills and abilities.

People & Planet - Reviewing my brainstorm of what people and planet need, and narrowing it down to one cohesive statement: that the *Opportunity to Prosper* is like an umbrella over *Accountable Leadership, Justice and Peace* and *How to Get On Track*. There three items are all required or are part of having more *Opportunity to Prosper*. The main theme here, *Opportunity to Prosper* also aligns with the foundation and principles of *service as our purpose*. "Justice" and "Peace", I think, are not necessarily connected, as peace is very much individually defined. Pursuing peace will be covered more in the next section, for now I will remove it from my list. This is getting interesting, assuming I am headed in the right direction. I think this statement is in tune with my feelings of the needs of people and planet: *My people and my planet need more opportunity to prosper.*

People and our planet need more solutions than any individual has answers. So, if you have multiple unconnected items, do away with those you don't feel you could dedicate an effort towards. Find the common theme with the remaining items, if more than one. What remains should be a need or desire of people or the planet that a product or service can meet. Can you see yourself getting behind such a product or service? If so, write a statement reflecting your belief in what people or the planet needs or desires without being specific about service or product. If not, either broaden your view of or reconsider what you feel people need. Write a statement.

Completing this exercise has probably aroused your enthusiasm for finding purpose and given you some insights. You may have started relating these elements to each other looking for that whole purpose, no? When relating these areas to each other, give consideration to how you manage these four key elements in your life today. More specifically, how does your positive or negative treatment of your pain affect your purpose. What happens if you don't follow your passion or you minimize your potential or not cater to the needs of others? Before you draw any conclusions, let's look at the positive and negative of each pair of pillars.

Pairing the Pillars for Perspectives on Purpose
Every pillar (white center boxes) can be matched with every other to provide valuable information about our

purpose. In the table below, we can find a range of possibilities that have extreme positive (light gray) and negative (darker gray) possible outcomes, depending on how we address or ignore these elements. Consider the six possible pillar pairs made horizontally, vertically and diagonally on the chart, to find the beneficial attributes as well as their possible distraction from our most meaningful purpose.

Leadership Opportunities	Service Missions	Personal Tools	Inspires People
Ego Based Pursuits	Pain	Passion	Path to Peace
Greed Based Pursuits	People	Potential	Path to Prosperity
Limits Growth	Perpetuates Problems	Limits Authenticity	Deters Leadership

■ Unconscious/Misdirected Approach ☐ Conscious/Purposeful Approach

Above Diagram: Keys and Clues of Combined Pairs

<u>Pain & Passion</u> have one really big thing in common - if they are not both being addressed productively, they will occupy a lot of time, thinking time. Without positively addressing pain, reminders of your pain will constantly pop up in daily life. The bad feelings and inappropriate reactions, stimulated by all kinds of outside influences, will cause dysfunction in a way that interrupts freedom of thought in the present. If not chasing passions, the mind will constantly expend energy thinking of getting back to that which is craved so much. You've heard it in others: the nagging fear in life or the book they want to write just will not let them have any peace. Yes, *peace*. These two pillars, pain & passion, are connected because they are directly related to attaining any measure of peace.

Addressing pain and chasing passions allows greater mind activity in the present, opening the door to living on purpose, the focus of this book. When pains are effectively dealt with, less conscious effort is spent judging the past. Passions, when not pursued will typically keep the mind focused on the future with worry about those things that can keep us from doing what we want.

Addressing pains and passions means to pursue the challenges associated with being stuck and prevents us to living our lives fully. Addressing our pains directly - identifying sources, reactions and beliefs - allows us to create new beliefs which will remove the obstacles of falsely held beliefs and judgements about ourselves. When working fully with passions, high energetic states are reached, the brain finds a desired healthy zone - homeostasis. Freed of pain and immersed in passion is a blissful state of mind, it is peace.

The two common approaches to pain and passion are ignoring and letting go. Both suggest pain and passion no longer exists or are successfully subdued. However, "letting go", often the goal in spiritual practice, counseling, and transformational techniques, is a commitment to working through the challenge of pain and finding the resistance that stops you from chasing your passions.

Attempts to "ignore" the regular stimulations that activate pain and passion are tantamount to believing that the fast moving train coming towards you, will not hurt you. In both cases, unaddressed pain and passion will eventually show up in some undesired fashion and limit your ability to manifest personal greatness in the present. (Greatness is the recognized element in you that is most worthy of consideration by, and benefit to, others.) Finding peace is best pursued off the tracks of fast moving trains.

Equally important, if you are actively challenged with pain and distracted from attending passions, the prospects of negatively affecting people and planet becomes a very real possibility. Delusional and egocentric actions are common responses to unaddressed pains and passions. A repetitive example of an extreme negative outcome, is witnessed every so often in our media as mass gun shootings. In every one of these cases, it is found that the perpetrators felt like outcasts or separated from the greater society. Their pain, as found by psychologists, was so great and unattended, they developed a passion to get revenge.

We are obligated in principle, as a society, to ensure every person has access to pursue plenty of what they need for survival, to meet individual need and to avoid sending anyone to such a distraught point. We can prevent such disasters from occurring by giving focus to our pain and following our passions. Looking back at my example:

My pain of feeling less than others, and believing that I am not as significant to mankind, can be positively addressed in conjunction with my passion for story-telling. I can use my desire to tell stories to review those occurrences in my life which may give me insights as to why I am not doing all that I can today. I could also work with a counselor for direction, get involved in some transformational activities and spend more time being meditative, all proven methods of relieving pain and moving into passions.

In dealing with my challenge and following passions in this way, I can make progress, feel better about where I am in this world and avoid harmful ego based pursuits. More importantly, if I am approaching pain and passion head on, I will find a higher level of peace.

What ideas come to mind when considering how to directly address pain and follow passion?

<u>People & Potential</u> connects the needs of people with one's natural talents, which ideally results in both personal prosperity and value to humanity. On the other end of the spectrum, the same pair can lead to greed when not in alignment with man's purpose to serve. In my example, potential - natural and learned gifts - is in bringing people and projects together for execution to meet people and planet needs for more opportunity to prosper, could turn to greed by simply using skills to take advantage of people's needs. As an example, I could use marketing skills to sell get rich quick schemes to fleece the needy and enhance my wealth, a common offering in a society bent on excessive greed.

In a more positive approach to my talents and peoples need, would be in working with members of my community to organize around a project for mutual benefit. My particular desire would be around creating more "opportunity to prosper" from farmers' markets to community based information to assist those who lack resources to gain the assistance needed to grow.

How can you use your inherent skills and abilities to meet your needs and those of others?

<u>People & Pain</u>, when combined, reveal the basis for personal missions of service. With an understanding of one's own pain, working with those experiencing the same or similar pain could lead to mass healing and massive steps in human evolution. Imagine the amplified effect of many addressing their pain and using it to serve others with the same problem.

Not recognizing the need to both positively address pain and serve the needs of others would perpetuate the pain and continue to separate people. For example, imagine a like-minded group suffering the same kind of misery from military drone strikes, might come together to promote damaging perceptions and end up forming a terrorist group, fomenting separation of people.

My positive example would be recognizing my pain of being discriminated against, as found in most groups of people, is an opportunity to serve others by helping them to identify, positively deal with by recognizing the false perceptions and eliminating made up stories and inherited beliefs. I can also help those unaware of this suffering, to become more sympathetic and sensitive to promote healing.

How could you positively address your torment and help others with similar feelings?

Potential & Passion represent the tools, mediums and methods that move one's purpose. The energy inherent in working with passions coupled with the potential of natural gifts combine as a powerhouse of efficient activity. Used affirmatively, expertise is unrestrained and available. Used negatively, these same elements will stifle great innovation, waste evolutionary growth, and can be used as tools to separate humanity.

My marketing skills and my passion for storytelling are tools capable of influencing people.

What tools, mediums & methods are available to you and how could they be used to serve you and humanity?

Potential & Pain pillars represents unique leadership opportunities when approached positively and utilized for the benefit of others. Such opportunities are lost when pain is left to fester or personal potential is used without consideration of impact to mankind.

Six Steps to Living On Purpose

Considering my skill set, I will demonstrate leadership by openly addressing my long endured pain by specifically communicating and seeking solutions wherever the opportunity presents itself.

How can you use your gifts to lead others in dealing with similar pain or your most empathetic feelings?

<u>People & Passions</u> come together as powerful inspiration for others, when properly delivered from the heart with passion. Expressed passion brings contagious enthusiasm, inspiring others to higher levels of conscious effort in any area of life. When we do not embrace our passions, they will lack luster to inspire and may even have the opposite affect on others. Overly egocentric driven passions may deter others from pursuing their own common passions out of fear they too may appear as egomaniacs.

My meaningful and passionately told stories of interest, told to those who can relate, could easily energize and inspire some beyond their current limits and into their own purpose.

How could your positive treatment of people & passions help meet your needs and humanity's?

Now, if you haven't, relate your four pillars of purpose in pairs to find more clues into your own purpose. Starting horizontally, how do your pains relate to your passions in finding personal *peace*? How can your potential skills meet needs of people and create your *prosperity*? Go through all six pairs to find big clues for your life's purpose.

Using Keys & Clues to Find Your Vision

Keys to your purpose consist of your four summarized statements from the brainstorm. Clues are from the pairing of pillars you just finished. By simply having all of this information in front of you, you should be able to begin to see a bigger picture of how these things come together. Here is the all-encompassing four part question that you will need to summarize your purpose:

How can you positively address your pain, fervently follow passions using your natural and learned skills to meet needs and desires of people while having a positive impact on humanity?

Six Steps to Living On Purpose

From my example, my keys are:
- Separated - less than others, not good enough
- Storytelling - speaking, writing, showing
- Team Builder - organizing, marketing, problem solving, communicating
- Need Opportunity - leadership, justice, direction

My clues are:
- Write stories about pain to understand and heal
- Organize & team building for meaningful projects
- Positively addressing common pain in groups
- Storytelling & marketing to make a difference
- Standing up, being open with every opportunity
- Tell meaningful stories to inspire & energize others

My feelings are:
- I want to eliminate the feeling of being separated from humanity for all, by;
- telling meaningful stories that inspire others to stand up and live purposely;
- bring together those prepared to create community projects to benefit all;
- offering greater opportunity to find peace and prosperity.

Play with your keys and clues. What's coming up for you? What are your feelings towards these revelations that you've always really known?

Writing Your Statement of Purpose

Feel your way into your purpose statement and keeping all aspects included, it should flow naturally. Remember, pain is at the heart of your purpose, but all pillars are being attended to here. You can break your statement into more than one sentence, if needed, or allow it to be a run on. What is important is that you feel it, own it, that it is a part of your authentic self.

You want your statement of purpose to be action and solution oriented but broad enough that you don't have to change it every time you take on a new mission. For example, I know I prefer to be project oriented, so rather than stating that my purpose is to "fight racial discrimination" I might use, "build bridges over the gaps that separate individuals and groups," keeping it action and solution oriented but broad enough so that I take up any form of separation. This purpose absorbs my specific pain and is broad enough to take on the pain of the handicap, ethnic or religious groups.

Next, my passion is all about "storytelling" so how about "I handle my purpose by telling meaningful and inspiring stories." My potential is zeroed in on "team building." Lastly I want to include people's needs. So, I have come up with this initial statement:

My purpose in life is to build bridges over those gaps that separate individuals and groups, to tell stories, build teams and meet needs.

Okay, that's a pretty dry statement. I want my purpose to be meaningful, inspiring, and arousing. I want more description and power in my statement. Maybe this:

My purpose in life is to build bridges over the gaps that separate people. I do this by facing my pain positively, telling powerful stories that inspire, maximizing my natural skills of organizing, marketing, team building and problem solving, to meet needs of people to have greater opportunity for peace and prosperity.

Write your statement of purpose, sit with it, rewrite it, sleep on it, and improve it. Read it aloud until it rolls off your tongue as smoothly as you wrote it. Embrace your final version of your purpose.

Knowing and Using Your Statement of Purpose

Your purpose in life represents you, it is your calling card, it stands when you are sleeping, your guiding light when you are awake and a beacon for those looking for your gifts. You created this purpose from a deep inner knowing of yourself, now emblazon it into your memory. State it and write it, first thing every morning until it is solidly memorized. Speak it every chance you get. State it at the beginning of any address. Recite it when someone asks you about yourself. Soon, if not immediately, you will find yourself standing taller, worthy of the purpose of your life. Your known purpose will keep you focused and serve to inspire others to live more purposeful lives.

In order to fully live a life of purpose, in alignment with man's principles or purpose, you will need to *positively address your pain, fervently follow your passion and maximize your potential to meet needs of people, while monitoring the impact your actions have on humanity.*

Your purpose will continue to change and mature as you live and experience new avenues in your life. Remain open to modify it as needed. Purposes do change in life and the younger you are, the more likely it will change as you learn more about yourself. That is not to say that you can't identify a purpose but to be open to change.

Use the space below and the back of book to write your statement of purpose till it feels good meets your need.

_____

_____

_____

_____

_____

_____

_____

_____

_____

_____

_____

_____

_____

_____

_____

_____

_____.

Summarizing Purpose

Living with purpose is an old concept, it is what we had to do without thinking. When we consciously identify and pursue a personal purpose in life we avoid being distracted and defaulting into an unconscious purpose. There were times when technology was not as prevalent, corporations not as dominant, and human beings worked with a great deal more conscious purpose. Ask a survivor of the depression or World War II years and you'll get a better sense of purposeful lives. Living with purpose has now become a necessity for all humankind as we approach climatical points of no return, energy challenges, food supply concerns along with a renewed sense of responsibility and justice for all of earth's inhabitants.

Survival of the human species is everyone's concern and responsibility. Leaving the big challenges of today in the hands of governments, corporations or anyone else to resolve, may ultimately prove irresponsible on our part. Living on purpose is self-empowering, inspires others, takes power back from those who use it for their purposes and it benefits all humanity.

"Your rewards in life are proportionate to the risks that you take!"

~ Anonymous

A couple of weeks into my program to remake my life, I decided to go back to school and enrolled in a Business Psychology class. The first day of class, the professor had us complete an assessment questionnaire. It was a simple psychological assessment with several yes/no, true/false and multiple choice questions.

The professor asked to speak to me for a minute, at the end of class. He explained the questionnaire was a stress test and mine had stood out when he was glancing through them. "Your assessment begs me to ask, "Did you answer the questions as honestly as possible, Mr. Taylor" he enquired.

"Yes."

"So, how are you doing, Mr. Taylor?" He asked gauging me carefully, looking for some clues to some theory, I imagined.

A bit dumbfounded, I responded with arched eyebrows, "I'm fine, why do you ask?

Again, the professor looked me over closely assessing my potential reaction to what he was about to say, and eased out his own assessment, "Well, I hope I'm not overstepping my bounds with you, but based on your responses to this assessment, you should be dead!"

"Dead?" I timidly smiled while my heart raced. Something in my responses to his questionnaire obviously. I didn't realize I was under stress - was I so out of touch with myself, walking through life in a daze? We talked and determined that my regular attendance to the gym, sometimes twice a day, was a huge stress reliever for me and that I should definitely continue. I was grateful for that assessment, I learned a lot about myself in the few minutes we spoke and that was the most valuable thing I remember from that class – my assessment!

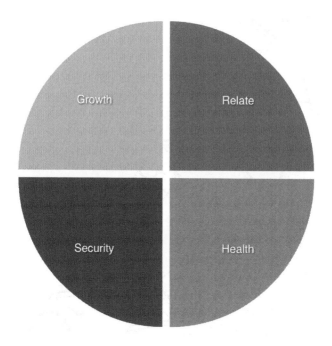

Step Three:
Assess Your Life Today

Imagine a huge map, of life with millions of possible destinations. Before you can begin your journey, you must determine two things: your destination and where you are on this map. The self assessment in this step three, will determine where you are located on this map of opportunity while step four is critical in determining your destination and mapping out a path to get there.

This step three is also important in selecting a program in step five and creating positive affirmations in step six. Your self assessment is where you begin to formulate a roadmap with your well thought through responses.

This may be your toughest of the six steps as it requires you to take a close look in the mirror. Self examination is challenging for all of us, as we are our own worse and best critics and often don't want to look at painful aspects of our lives. This process, when done with integrity, will have the greatest impact in the tailoring of your transformational program that ultimately dictates where you will go, when and how you'll get there and what you'll get on arrival.

There are four major sections in this assessment, each one consists of three areas to be answered totaling twelve specific aspects of your life. There are only twenty-two actual assessment questions. The questions leading up to the assessment questions in bold are there to prompt thought and need not be answered at that point. Answer only the 22 questions in **bold** print.

This self assessment should be a reasonable reflection of where you are in your life, which is important in defining a starting point on your life's roadmap. This assessment should be completed in one sitting with your responses coming right after each reviewed topic. There are no right or wrong answers, only truthful or reliable ones.

Purpose

Purpose is the reason you are here, the point of your existence or your justification for holding this book in hand. Having read the previous chapter, you should know your purpose. If not, this rating should reveal that you need to step back and more clearly define your purpose.

With purpose in mind, consider these questions:
- *How well do you know your purpose? Can you clearly state your purpose?*
- *Is your purpose of any value to others? Do you fill a need or a desire with your purpose?*
- *How much time is spent pursuing your purpose? Is it a full time effort or is it still in the formulation stages?*

- *Is following your purpose providing income? Can it ever cover your expenses? In order to pursue your purpose, does it need to cover your expenses?*
- *Do you have a plan to live your purpose? Do you know what to do to live your purpose?*

Rating scale: 0 - 10

0 = no clue as to my purpose;

10 = I clearly know my purpose, I am completely immersed in and love my purpose, I work at it full time, it is a gift to others, and I am financially rewarded for it.

How well do you know your purpose? ____

Relationships

Relationships with people may not rank as your highest priority but for most it is a requirement for living. Here, you will evaluate your relationships with those you are likely to encounter regularly. This area does not include a significant other, which is found in "Love Partnering".

You may replace areas to be evaluated that do not apply to you, with other individuals or groups of significance. For example, if you are an only child, you may want to replace the "Siblings" area with another more vital bond such as a "Mentor", "Club Members" or "Teammates".

You will be rating in several areas independent of each other. For each group, rate according to where the relationship is today, using the rating system below. You may use whole numbers or fractions between 0 and 10. In the case of relationships that you desire to have, where there is little or no communication, such as with a deceased or an estranged person, the rating would be "0." If there is a relationship you do not have such as, an only child without "Siblings" give a rating of "10."

How to Rate Your Relationships	
A relationship is desired but does not exist, or there is no communication whatsoever.	0.0
There are strained or hostile communications.	2.0
Relationship is limited, difficult to build.	4.0
There is communication with a limited understanding & agreement but potential.	6.0
There is good communication, understanding and common ground.	8.0
The relationship is perfect, nonexistent or not desired.	10

Relationship Notes:

Consider how you interact with "Other People Regularly Encountered" such as neighbors, postal workers, police, wait staff, cashiers, etc. "Interactions with Strangers" could be that person standing in line behind you at the grocery store or someone who asks you a question while passing on the street. How do you relate in these random meetings?

Your relationship with "The Earth" pertains to how you relate to the environment, plant and animal life. Are all living things essential to life on this planet and do you make personal efforts to maintain them? (Rate it a "0" if you feel nature does fine on its own, not involved with saving anything, recycling, etcetera and kill unwanted things in your space. Rate it a "10" if you feel "the planet is part of your responsibility, and make every effort to sustain life as one of our vital issues today).

Your relationship to a "Higher Power" is how you relate to God, infinite intelligence, universal law, science, Darwinism, etcetera. This is not reserved to religion or science but to your own beliefs and how you relate to those beliefs. Rate based on your clarity of understanding of those beliefs.

How would you rate the quality of your relationship with:	
Children	
Siblings	
Parents	
Grandparents	
Friends	
Coworkers & Associates	
Other People Regularly Encountered	
Interaction with Strangers	
The Earth	
Higher Power	
Total Assessed Relations Rating	

After rating of each group, add the scores together and enter as the "Total Assessed Relations Rating." Then divide that total by 10, to scale with the other ratings. This number is your overall relationship rating.

What is your overall assessment rating? ____

Love Partnering

Partnering in a loving relationship is the most significant of all relationships you are likely to have in life. Choosing a mate is one of the few opportunities where you get to pick the other party in relationship. If you want to be in a relationship but are not in one, evaluate your most recent. If you are not in such a relationship and do not want to be, rate this a "10" and move on.

Consider these things before answering:
- *Why are you or why do you want to be in a loving relationship (love, security, habit, children, etc.)?*
- *How open, honest and easy are your communications?*
- *How much would you like your partner to change?*
- *How much do you sacrifice for love (career, passion, hobbies, quality of life, lifestyle, etc.)?*
- *How vulnerable can you be with your partner?*

- *How compatible do you feel with your partner (values, sexuality, health, activities, intellect, etc.)?*
- *Are there improvements you can make alone to create a more loving relationship?*

Rating scale: 0 - 10
 0 = you shouldn't be in the same room together;
10 = you are not in or have any desire to be in a loving relationship or have a great relationship.

How do you rate your love partnering? _____

Personal Development

We all have goals, from finding a way to work at our passions, to finding a partner. We may not have our goals formalized or consciously seek them, but we do move in the general direction of what we have impressed upon the mind as goals. Our casual approach to reaching loosely defined goals with a vague roadmap to getting us there is haphazard at best. By understanding, planning and taking definitive steps towards our goals, we can predictably and successfully meet the biggest of challenges.

Personal development involves preparing for the pursuit of your goals and improving the probability of reaching your most desired destinations in life. Consider these questions on your preparedness to reaching goals.

Consider these things before answering:
- *Do you have written goals?*
- *Do you have or have you ever created a plan for life?*
- *Have you identified aids to reaching your goals?*
- *Have you received any training towards your goals?*
- *Are your job and purpose closely related?*
- *Are you doing anything to improve your ability to pursue your purpose freely?*
- *Have you consciously rid yourself of bad habits?*
- *Have you consciously created any new habits?*
- *Have you willfully changed your life in the past?*

Rating scale: 0 - 10
 0 = I have no clue what I am doing;
10 = I have a great plan and moving in the specific direction to reach my goals.

How do you rate your overall level of personal development today? ____

Health

Health, for assessment purposes, is divided into emotional, physical and dietary health. Emotional health can be measured and defined by how well one remains in a reasoning mode in adverse situations, under stress or unfamiliar circumstances to how well one responds or expresses emotions of love, joy, affection and passion.

Physical health pertains to the state of your bodily functions and capabilities. Dietary health is what, when and how we consume food to benefit the body. Life can run a lot easier when we have these systems sorted out as best possible!

Be completely honest about where you stand today and it will be a lot easier to plot how to get where you want to be tomorrow. Mental health has been purposely avoided in this assessment as it requires the knowledge of a professional mental health worker. If you suspect that you may be dealing with mental health issues, please contact a professional.

Emotional Health

In assessing emotional health, think of holding fear and love at opposite ends of the spectrum. All emotions boil down to being on one side or the other—love or fear. Think about the wide range of emotions to different situations and consider if they are based in fear or love. Hint: Jealousy is not based in love but is the fear of losing love, just in case you were wondering. Think it through.

Consider these things before answering:
- *How often are you filled with a sense of love, joy, gratitude and appreciation?*
- *How well do you express your love, joy, gratitude and appreciation to others?*
- *What fears do you have? Can you identify your fears?*
- *How well do you manage fears? (flying, bugs, tight spaces, strange people, etc)*
- *Do you have any tools, techniques or methods to overcome your fears? Do you use them successfully?*
- *How well do you handle surprises and emergencies?*
- *How do fears or emotions affect your job or relationship with others?*
- *How do you move beyond a negative emotional state?*

- *How well do you manage your emotional challenges (jealousy, depression, self-criticism, inability to forgive, judgement of others, etcetera)?*
- *Do you ever purposely challenge yourself and go outside of your comfort zone?*

Rating scale:

0 = fear dominates my life;

10 = love dominates my life.

How would you rate your emotional health? ____

Physical Health

How well your body functions and endures can play a significant role in quality of life, longevity, and reaching your planned destinations.

Consider these things before answering:

- *Do you have chronic health problems? If so, do they prevent you from activities you want to participate?*
- *Do you take medication regularly? If so, do they prevent you from desirable activities?*
- *Do you have any unaddressed health issues?*
- *Do you get 20 minutes of aerobic exercise at least 3 times a week?*

- *Do you have any disabilities that limit activities?*
- *Do you maximize participation in physical activities?*
- *Is your physical health improvable?*
- *Do you have a plan to maintain your physical health?*

Rating scale:

0 = worst possible physical condition, death is at the door and or incapable of independent mobility;

10 = the absolute best of physical health.

How would you rate your physical health? ____

Dietary Health

What, when and how much you eat are important to physical health. How in tune to diet are you?

Consider these things before answering:

- *Are you consciously aware of what you are eating?*
- *Are you conscious of how much you eat? Do you often feel like you've eaten too much? Do you eat fast?*
- *Are you conscious of your daily water intake?*
- *How often do you eat fast food?*
- *Do you eat 3 planned meals a day?*
- *Do you abuse tobacco, alcohol or sugar?*
- *Do you often consume food outside of regular meals?*

- Do you often skip meals or eat when not hungry?
- Do you plan when you will eat your meals?
- Are you conscious of food choices when shopping?
- Have you confirmed the need to take supplements?
- How much do you know about nutritional needs?

Rating scale:

0 = no knowledge about nutrition and eat whatever is convenient when I'm hungry;

10 = completely aware of modern nutrition and maintain a healthy diet to meet my needs.

How would you rate your dietary health? ____

Community & World Relations

Our contributions or gifts to the world are most often subtle, we may not even recognize those things that are of value to others. We might be surprised by the effects we have on the world from the smallest things we do and say. Think of the things you write and say to people that could be repeated, both positive and negative. Facebook is a great example of how things can be passed along repeatedly that can have an impact on the consciousness of the world. Your gift, is something special from you that fills a need or desire of others.

<u>Consider these things before answering:</u>
- *What gifts do you regularly give to others?*
- *Do you have a way of giving aid to others?*
- *How do you interact with people who cross your path?*
- *Are you involved in community activities or projects?*
- *Do you volunteer your special gifts when needed?*
- *Do you stand up for what's right when it's needed?*
- *When there is opportunity to work with others, are you driven to inspire?*
- *What do you do to make this world a better place?*
- *If your every word and action was immediately felt by the entire world, would you have an overall good or bad impact on the world?*

Rating scale:
 0 = my words and actions would have 100% bad impact on my community and world;
10 = my words and action would have 100% good impact on my community and world.

How would you rate you impact on your community and world today? _____

Subsistence Source

Your subsistence source is from what or where you get what you need to live. This could include a job, your passionate work, retirement funds, government welfare program, prison, farming, family or a trust fund. The source does not have to provide you with money but the means by which you survive.

Consider these things before answering:
- *How dependable is your subsistence source?*
- *Do you to maintain 6-12 months of living expenses?*
- *Is the source of a permanent nature?*
- *Does the source allow you to pursue your purpose?*
- *How happy are you with this source?*
- *Would you like to improve or replace this source?*
- *Does this source meet all of your needs?*

Rating scale:
0 = if you have no subsistence source whatsoever;
10 = if you have, without concern of ever losing your subsistence source.

How would you rate your subsistence source? ____

Future Stability

Your future stability is what you have to fall back on if things fell apart at any time. If you suddenly lost your job or subsistence source, how prepared are you to manage without your primary subsistence source? Your secondary subsistence source could include: savings, relatives, friends, home or other salable assets.

Consider these things before answering:

- *If you lost your primary subsistence source, could you survive six months to a year on your own?*
- *Could you thrive the rest of your life on your secondary source?*
- *How difficult would it be to survive without your primary subsistence source?*
- *Do you have a plan B, in the event you lost primary subsistence source?*
- *Is your secondary source immediately accessible? Would you have to sell something to support yourself?*
- *Can you depend on friends or family to support you temporarily if you were incapable?*
- *Do you have personal survival skills if things really fell apart? (Hunting, farming, gathering, etc.)*

- Do you have survival skills of value to others? (Make electricity, grow food, build a structure, etc.)

Rating scale:

0 = no secondary source, survival skills or anyone you can depend and poor health;

10 = I am absolutely taken care of in any kind of event for as long as necessary.

How would you rate your future stability? ____

Dominant Environments

Your dominant environments do not necessarily have to be work and home though they are in most cases. A traveling sales person might find themselves evaluating the quality of the hotels they regularly stay, and a fisherman might have to judge the boat they are captive on for months at a time. Wherever you spend large blocks of time can qualify as your dominant or primary environments. Rate the quality of such environments.

Consider these things before answering:

- Are you comfortable in your dominant work and play environments?

- Are your environments healthy and safe?

- If possible, would you change these environments?
*- Are you exposed to uncontrollable circumstances and
  situations in your primary spaces?*

Rating scale:

0 = environments are not healthy and can't be changed;

10 = perfect environments that I can change at anytime.

How would you rate your dominant or primary environments? ____

Exposure, Travel & Vacation

Exposure to environments that are beyond your familiar boundaries changes your perspective, can generate new thought patterns, stimulate change and relax the mind from its daily challenges. Changes in environments can produce dramatic changes in feelings. If you live in a city with lots of pavement and concrete, getting into a forest can prove to be a big stimulus for change and vice versa. A hike in nature can shift mindset for anyone working indoors all day. Vacationing in a foreign culture can support dramatic change, travel opens eyes and doors and weekend getaways can wipe away a week of stress.

<u>Consider these things before answering:</u>
- *Do you get outside of everyday environments often?*
- *Do you take vacations to foreign environments?*
- *Do you go away from primary environments long enough to relax, forget about work, before returning?*
- *Do you spend your days off living outside of your box?*
- *Do you seek out places to visit for their differences or their similarities to your normal surroundings?*

Rating scale:
0 = I never leave my environment and don't desire to;
10 = I regularly get exposed to new environments and can relax from everyday challenges.

How would you rate your exposure, travel and vacation? _____

_____

<u>Summarizing Your Assessment</u>

Congratulations! Your self assessment is complete, if you rated the 12 areas of your life. The completed assessment is a definition of where you are today in this world. Having identified where you are makes it a lot easier to create a map to where you want to go. Before you begin defining where it is you want to go, let's get a visual of where you are now.

In the following sample assessment, I have shaded the areas of my chart to correspond to my ratings. This gives me a perfect visual of my life and allows me to easily find areas that are out of balance with the rest. Imagine this to be a wheel intended to roll smoothly. You can easily identify the part of life that would make this wheel very difficult to roll.

You may note, all scores are less than 10 because I feel there is always room for improvement. This certainly does not need to be your practice, it is more important to be consistent throughout your evaluation. First answers tend to be the most accurate, so, if you didn't complete your assessment in one sitting, now is the time to review just your final rating in each area for consistency.

In this example, the areas of subsistence source, future stability and community & world relations are far from being balanced with the other areas. My objective is to balance the wheel so that it can roll smoothly. In the next section, goals will be written based on this wheel summary.

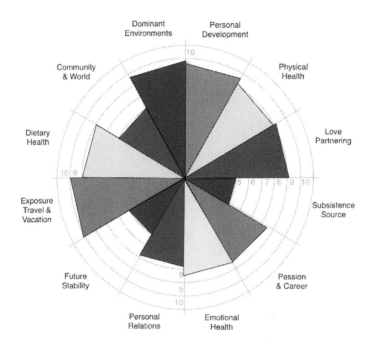

Figure 1. Example Summary Wheel

Now, with a pencil, shade in your ratings from the assessment to get a visual of your life. This will make it easy to pick out the areas of your life that you'll want give a little more focus in the next steps of planning, programming and affirming.

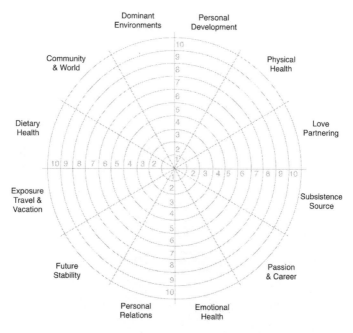

Figure 2. Blank Summary Wheel

You likely had a sense of where you were in this world before completing your assessment, this is merely a visual representation of your life's balance. On the map of life, you have pinpointed where you are today. In the next step, we will determine your destination and then define milestones on the map in detail. If you aren't excited at this point, go back to step 2, listen to more audio programs as often as possible then get some fuel, almost time to hit the road.

"The most dangerous risk of all - The risk of spending your life not doing what you want on the bet you can buy yourself the freedom to do it later."

~ Randy Komisar

Six Steps to Living On Purpose

I once had a friend who irresponsibly told me, at my ripe age of 17, that I would die at an early age. It was a terrible thing to hear from a person I admired and respected. Strangely enough, it turned out to be a blessing in disguise as it forced me to focus on making everyday count and to live a more purposeful life.

Do you ever wonder if you are doing the right things in life? Ever feel like you are just drifting along and not making a difference in anything? Just surviving? Or, just not sure of your direction?

Every now and then when I am bored, in a melancholy state of mind, and lacking luster, I ask myself: "If I only had one year to live, what would I be doing?" I then compare that answer with what I am doing. If they aren't pretty close to being the same thing, I know that I'm doing something wrong. You don't know how much time you have, take advantage of the moment.

L. Leonard Taylor

Step Four:
Determine Where You Want To Be Tomorrow By Beginning With The End In Mind Today - Plan Life One Goal at a Time

I have listened to numerous motivational speakers and there is one thing they have in common—they believe *we must have goals*. Why do we need goals? Goals are the places we want to go in life, the people we want to be and the things we want to do - our destinations! We always have goals whether we consciously set them or not, they are how we arrived where we are today, however indirectly. In this step, we will purposely write goals to take us to specific places.

Motivational and inspirational speakers also agree that *we must write down our goals* to engrain them. When we write things down, we begin to give form to our thoughts which gives us a visual and builds memory. For years, educators and mind scientists have known that a student taking notes in class is far more likely to remember information from the class session than a student not taking notes, even if the writer never reads the notes again. Studies have also shown that those with written goals have gone farther in life and accomplished more than those who have not. When consciously set, written goals minimize uncertainty, and subconsciously keep goals in focus.

If you have read the chapter on goals in Stephen Covey's book, *Seven Habits of Highly Effective People,* you are well prepared for this section and understand the idea of writing goals by beginning with the end in mind. In his book, Covey suggests you imagine observing your own memorial service and consider what you would want friends, relatives, associates and others to say about you. Defining what you would want others to say can then take the form of seeing that very same person you want to be by the time you reach that destination. This would be a good time to ask yourself "Is this a greed or ego based goal or something that will truly benefit others?"

Try Covey's method, if you will. However, if you have your own process for writing your goals, please go with it! Writing your goals is key, not the process, though I strongly recommend you:

1) create at least one goal in each of the 12 areas of your life as found in the assessment;

2) make at least one additional goal to any deficient area identified in your assessment and;
write S.M.A.R.T. goals.

The S.M.A.R.T. way to write a goal includes:

1) Be very **S**pecific about what you plan to achieve;

2) Make sure the goal is **M**easurable;

3) The goal must be **A**chievable and **A**ction oriented;

4) Should be focused on the **R**esults and;

5) A **T**imeframe for completion.

You have completed your assessment, you have an idea of where you want to go and you know what a goal should consist of, right? If so, do not delay, start writing. Of course, you can find all kinds of methods on the Internet, just get the goals written! You probably already have a few goals in mind, so write them now and avoid spending time on the Internet. For those of you desiring a more detailed process, follow my process.

How I Create Goals

Essentially, I use six steps to creating goals:

  1) Create life mission statements for my 12 areas of life.

  2) Keeping assessment questions in mind, brainstorm ideas for goals in each area.

  3) Combine and eliminate ideas to come up with solid concepts for each area.

  4) Write S.M.A.R.T. goals with boiled down concepts.

  5) Break big goals down to attainable smaller goals.

  6) Post goals where they can be seen regularly.

I start by creating or updating a life long mission statement from each area of my life (the same 12 areas found in the assessment). Beginning with the end in mind, and my most out of balance area of life, in this case "Subsistence Source", I write what I'd want others to say and believe about me at my memorial. I take those thoughts, and compose them into a simple mission statement. The subsistence source mission statement is a reflection of how I want to be remembered by my community as it applies to how I supported myself. I try to keep the mission statement simple, not too wordy or too detailed. Goals give all the definition needed. Note: The mission statement should encompass every goal. Or, if you prefer, every goal should be in alignment with the mission statement.

<u>Mission Statement for "Subsistence Source"</u>:
Develop products and services that serve the needs of people while generating a fair income to meet my needs and those of any employees.

With a mission statement intact, focus on writing goals with the idea of keeping them aligned with the life mission. Write goals the S.M.A.R.T. way and break larger goals into reasonably attainable smaller goals. The "considerations" written before each assessment rating, in step three, are helpful in prompting new thoughts for goals. Rereading these considerations and keeping the mission in mind, write and rewrite goals until you have some worthy well defined goals.

Take whatever goals that appear to be overwhelming tasks and break them into smaller goals. In some cases, as in the example below, goals might be broken down several times to make them manageable and easily attained milestones:

GOAL: *Self publish and market my book, "Six Steps to Living On Purpose" by end of 2014.*

1. *Research the requirements of self publishing. (7 days)*
2. *Get necessary funding to self publish. (30 days)*
3. *Identify ways to improve the product/service and or broaden its scope, value & audience. (3 days)*
4. *Write business plan for self publishing. (21 days)*
5. *Develop a marketing strategy with predictable sales. (14 days):*
    1. *brainstorm & list product values (day 1);*
    2. *define target market (day 2);*
    3. *determine position with competition (day 3);*
    4. *identify how to promote (day 4);*
    5. *determine fair marketable price (day 5);*
    6. *identify placement to sell (day 6);*
    7. *create one cohesive document (day 14).*
6. *Create timeline for implementation. (7 days)*

Big goals require more steps. Any goal can be reached one step at a time. Zig Zigler likes to say, "You can eat an elephant one bite at a time!" Take on your big dreams, one bite at a time.

Write your goals, review them regularly, work them earnestly. Keep goals in front of you with goal boards. Bulletin, cork, white and magnetic boards can make tracking goals easier, keeping goals a priority and reaching goals faster.

Twelve Goal Setting Tips
1) Write down your known goals first.
2) Block out your life into the 12 assessment areas and place known goals in appropriate areas.
3) Write lifelong mission statements for each category by beginning with the end in mind.
4) Reread the *considerations* found in your assessment and brainstorm for possible goals.
5) Combine and eliminate ideas to specifications of writing S.M.A.R.T. goals.
6) Breakdown large goals to bite size smaller goals.
7) Make a timeline for goals, from days to months to years as needed.

8) Use meaningful points in time like birthdays, end of a particular year, etc. for long term goals.

9) Keep the goals aligned with lifelong mission statements.

10) Keep goals handy and visible: goal board, 3x5 cards, notebook, screensaver, etc.

11) Write goals at least once a year, then add, change or delete goals at any time.

12) Keep at least one goal for every area of your life.

Summary of Goal Setting

Considering the weight of this effort to plan your life, treat this with the importance that you have for your life. What the mind can manifest is only limited by the things you can imagine, which also means that undesired goals can manifest themselves when given undue attention. Be careful of what you ask. Creating a life map is a major step for planning the life you want to unfold and puts you in a unique group—less than 10% of all people. Congratulations!

Six Steps to Living On Purpose

With subliminal suggestion and self hypnosis, "Changes will take place in your life as they should, without effort, without thought, without strain."

~ Barrie Konicov

There were many things that needed fixing when I decided to make a new life. From my personal development point of view, I lacked the confidence to pursue many of my goals. My lack of confidence was due to low self-esteem or poor self-image and it was severely limiting the most important areas of my life.

The quieting of the daily noise, in step one, helped to clear my head. The new mind food of step two gave me unbelievable hope that I could become a different person. Steps three and four helped me to understand who I was, where I stood in this world, and put me on the road to discovery. However, not until I found the tools to change some unwanted behavior and build my confidence, was I able to take the wheel of my vehicle and begin moving down that road.

Through the tools of subliminal persuasion and self-hypnosis, I bypassed the need for the psychoanalysis of the "whys," which could be a lifelong endeavor. In addressing the need for healthier behavior, I allowed myself to leap beyond my limitations and directed my life in the pursuit of my passions and goals. I am grateful for the exposure to these tools that thrust me forward in reconstruction of my life.

Step Five:
Subliminal Suggestion and Self-Hypnosis: Programming Your Unconscious Mind

Step five uses both subliminal suggestion and self-hypnosis to help move you beyond fears and big challenges. These tools will aid in changing behavior by bringing your subconscious or unconscious mind into alignment with your conscious goals and desires, without great effort. The resulting programming will engrain beliefs, focus attention and be the quiet assistant working in your best interest.

Subliminal suggestion, also referred to as subliminal persuasion, subliminal programming or subliminal messaging, is a method of feeding the subconscious or unconscious, information without the conscious mind being aware. Subliminal programming can be delivered audibly when mixed with music or other sounds. Subliminal programming can also be conveyed visually through undetectable images or words embedded in a video or film. When subliminal messages are delivered audibly or visually to the mind, they are below the conscious threshold and therefore not subject to conscious scrutiny and discrimination.

"Self-hypnosis" is self-induced hypnosis which has been loosely and widely interchanged with the word "auto-suggestion" in the personal development industry. Auto-suggestion, which is similar in nature to positive affirmations that will be discussed in the next step, is the repetitive use of verbal statements, designed to change behavior. For our purposes, "self-hypnosis" and "auto-suggestion" are being used in conjunction with each other. Self-hypnosis is being used in this step to put the subject in a relaxed state and then deliver auto-suggestive statements repetitively to change unwanted behavior and to create new behavior.

Self-hypnosis has been an accepted therapeutic practice since it's inception early in the 20th century. Subliminal suggestion, on the other hand, has been the subject of ongoing debate in advertising and academic circles as to its effectiveness. Advertisers insists that subliminal messaging does not work after federal regulators sought to control or ban its use to sell products. Today, millions of people find self-hypnosis effective in bringing about their desired results. One only needs to look at the movies to observe the paid product placement to know that subliminal suggestion is used in American media.

In a customized program, subliminal suggestion and self-hypnosis delivers coordinated statements, maximizing the effectiveness of your program. A subliminal suggestion program conveys statements subconsciously and can be listened to at any time. Self-hypnosis uses similar content as the subliminal suggestion but encourages deep relaxation, allowing the mind to absorb the material with ease. Positive affirmations, discussed in step six, are stated with conscious awareness, at specific times for specific purposes. The messages are similar in all modes and extremely effective when used together.

You can create your own customized subliminal and self hypnosis programs. Should you decide to create your own recordings, first read the step six on creating affirmations to build effective affirmations that should be used in your recordings. Also consider using music from the baroque period, as it is perfectly suited for putting you into a heightened state of learning. Perform an Internet search for website links that can help create your own subliminal recordings and teach you to self hypnotize. Creating your own custom recordings is not necessary for a good program, as there are experts in this field that make such programs.

There are dozens of companies that produce subliminal and self-hypnosis programs. However, few make professional programs of both subliminal suggestion and self-hypnosis that work together. To select an audio program, consider your more important goals in conjunction with personal development goals. Look for a common thread between them that will allow you to find a fitting program. For example, a shy person with a goal to be more assertive in finding a partner might tie this desire to a personal development goal to get over a fear of public speaking. Perhaps a program on either public speaking or self confidence would be a good fit for overall more confident communications.

Barrie Konicov, a leading hypnotherapist, and his company, *Potentials Unlimited*, have built a solid reputation and library of audio programs. This company offers the widest selection of audio programs with both self-hypnosis and subliminal suggestion in one program, and are the only trusted source I can recommend. They have agreed to offer readers of this book their program on "self confidence" at a 75% discount. (See details at end of this chapter). This program was selected because it is in high demand, very effective and perfect for anyone wanting to make any kind of change in life. Regardless of your level of confidence, this program will help build courage and strengthen your will to make change real in your life.

For those desiring a different program, consider programs made on cassette tapes from Potentials Unlimited as they are the least expensive medium for about $6, at time of this books release. They also have CDs and downloadable mp3s. Regardless of the programs you decided on, listen to your programs daily and whenever possible. I suggest listening to your *self-hypnosis* version at bedtime and at any time you need to reduce stress except when driving. The more you listen to your *subliminal recording*, which can be listened to while driving, the greater the benefit.

Within days of implementing this step in your program in conjunction with steps one and two, you will begin to feel empowered in your quest for transformation. You have already begun to change and will continue to progress towards your goals. The force is with you now and your will is stronger each time you listen to any of your self subscribed audio programs.

Recommended Program from Potentials Unlimited:
Self Confidence #05, SCII Baroque Music, SKU115SC. Downloadable version for Apple products, mp3 players or any computer. $6.25. As of, September, 2014 it is regularly priced at $24.96. PLEASE NOTE: You must enter code "LT2012" to receive the discount! The price is subject to change as I have no control over Potentials Unlimited nor do I receive any financial benefit. Access at: http://potentialsunlimited.com

Self-Hypnosis Link:
http://www.mindtools.com/stress/
RelaxationTechniques/SelfHypnosis.htm

"All that a man achieves and all that
he fails to achieve is the direct
result of his thoughts."

~ James Allen
"As A Man Thinketh"

Step Six:
Negative Messages, Self-Talk and
Positive Affirmations

Researchers say we are bombarded daily with thousands of negative messages from media, encounters with people and our own self-talk. These messages, as subtle as "...the stock market fell today," as simple as someone stating, "...the world is going to hell" or as blatantly self abusive as, "I can be such an idiot", come at us relentlessly all day long. These compounded messages can leave us with a pessimistic view of life, leading to apathy, helplessness and even depression. Step six, will focus on effectively neutralizing negative messages and developing positive beliefs with pre-planned, well thought-through affirmations.

Like the promises of step five, when messages are repeatedly heard or spoken, they become thoughts. Repeated thoughts becomes beliefs. Beliefs shape behavior. Behavior become habits and habits become part of our character. This should be all the motivation needed to move us toward controlling the flow of unwanted messages by building our own regular diet of positive messages. In step one we cut the regular diet of media. In steps two and five we began filling the void of negative messages with inspirational, motivational and specific positive messages. However, to combat the negative messages from uncontrollable sources, we must take a more vigilant and conscious approach using positive affirmations.

Affirmations are statements written to support or change an existing belief or build a new belief. A belief is an idea that has become one's truth. However, one's truth is not a fact but a leap of faith as a result of being told, hearing, speaking or thinking repeatedly. Affirmations are tools that reinforce, create or change beliefs through repetitive use and can be positive or negative. Consciously affirming positive statements, when used in conjunction with subliminal suggestion and self hypnosis, will effectively neutralize negative messages and can turn self talk from an enemy to a supporter of your wishes!

Self-talk is a powerful programmer and is a form of affirmation, good or bad. Self-talk, those little things that we say to ourselves on a regular basis, can be negative and have detrimental effects on what we believe about ourselves and life. When consciously aware, we can use positive affirmations in our self-talk to build positive beliefs about ourselves rather than undermine our best intentions.

Affirmations are the perfect tool to use when we are dealing with unexpected, uncontrollable situations fraught with negativity. In an instant of reaffirming what we believe, we can also neutralize unsolicited negative judgments and reaffirm an associated positive. Affirmations are powerful tools to change our regular conversations with ourselves when we are aware of our own self-talk. We can easily change our auto responses and beliefs from a negative to a positive with a little monitoring. Time and repetition can change our thoughts, actions, habits and even character.

Creating meaningful affirmations begins with identifying where they are needed. Consider:
    1) Lower rated assessment areas.
    2) Recurring themes that showed up in the assessment and goal creation areas.
    3) Daily challenges with people and situations.

4) Easily identified derogatory self-talk statements.

5) Things you have a sheer desire to change.

Affirmations work best when they are tailored for your particular needs. For this reason, dig into your self assessment and look for recurring themes, challenges and thoughts. Then consider the daily challenges encountered on the job, in school, with family or those places you spend significant time. What messages are in direct conflict with your goals and desires and where do they come from? What are those people in your life saying that don't resonate with you? What affirmations would counteract these negatives?

Last but not least, what are you saying to yourself regularly? What are you saying to yourself in uncomfortable situations? What are you saying to yourself when you have to listen to others that you don't agree with? What are you saying when you are doing something you dislike doing? What are you saying to yourself when you make a mistake, do something wrong or say something embarrassing? What will you say to yourself that would neutralize these thoughts?

I suggest you consider the number of statements you can effectively memorize. You can memorize a lot more than what you might think. These are a few simple rules for writing affirmations that are powerful and life changing:

1) Use one voice – write all affirmations in either the first, second or third person.   I AM
2) Write them in present tense.
3) Make them short and specific: one subject, one verb & one adjective is usually best but not a hard and fast rule.
4) Avoid words like "try, no, don't, if, maybe, might, possibly", that are not definitively positive.
5) Use emotion, when possible, in your statements.

When you believe you have a reasonable affirmation repeat it a few times. The statement should roll off your tongue easily, comfortably. Can you make the flow better? Can you make the statement more meaningful, positive, powerful or specific? Your initial statement isn't likely to be your final one, though creating your affirmation will be a rewarding process. Here are a few sample affirmations relating to my speaking and personal development goals:

- I create opportunities to speak.
- I am focused & present when listening to others.
- I can recite the things that I believe in.
- I am kind and thoughtful with my words.
- I keep things simple when speaking to others.
- I openly share my knowledge when I have the opportunity to aid another.
- I am relaxed when I have the opportunity to speak.
- I radiate love with my smile.

Other examples of good affirmations.
- I keep a lean attractive body. (health)
- My body is responsive and free. (health)
- I have energy to use and to give. (health)
- I study hard and comprehend fast. (development)
- I am resourceful and get what I need. (career)
- I keep the commitments I make. (development)
- I have a healthy active lifestyle. (health)
- I choose to eat healthy food. (health)
- I build strong healthy relationships.(relationships)
- I am passionate about challenging work. (passion)

- I excel at operating with integrity. (career)
- I am disciplined in my work effort. (career)
- I love my inspirational work. (passion)
- I easily find creative solutions to challenging problems. (development)
- My wisdom grows with each day. (relationships)
- I meet each challenge with loving care. (development)
- I am constantly growing in all that I do. (development)
- I am grateful for being able to live a life of purpose. (spiritual)

Positive affirmations are to be memorized for easy recall and use. I keep at least one affirmation in every area of my life found in the assessment. I focus more on my personal development goals which usually call for some kind of behavior modification. I create and memorize my affirmations by writing and stating them everyday. I have included this ritual into my morning routine so that there is always time for them. I start with a pad, pen and list of my goals.

My process for creating and memorizing affirmations:

1. I write or rewrite each affirmation daily until memorized and keep them on a 3" x 5" just in case I forget any.
2. I check that I have listed all affirmations by counting or looking at an earlier list.
3. I will add or drop an affirmation whenever something is revealed to me and appropriate.
4. I state each affirmation three times with a different emphasis, enthusiasm and firmness.
5. I repeat this process every morning until I have a solid list of good affirmations.
6. When driving or I have an idle moment, I repeat all affirmations from memory, three times and refer to the card when I do not have total recall.

The repetition of writing, rewriting and reading will ensure you have created solid, meaningful and easily spoken affirmation while committing them to memory.

When and How to Use Affirmations

There will be times that you will be in the midst of contrasting beliefs and you will be very much aware of the uncontrollable negative utterances from the media and people you face daily. These are the moments where your affirmations will reject notions and beliefs not of your own thinking. When these opportunities present themselves it will be easy to pull from your memorized list of affirmations the perfect one to repeat to yourself three times or even interject into the conversation, if appropriate. Suddenly, we are consciously aware of the world around us, and it is more tolerable, more manageable and easier to navigate while heading to our destination.

There have been times in my life when the anxiety was very high. Usually, I found myself lying in bed with disturbing judgements of things of the past or worrying how something else would turnout in the future. It wasn't until I discovered the power of affirmations that I was able to confidently putdown a damaging view of life and find peace in the moment and completely place me on a positive track for the night or day.

Your affirmations are now your primary positive defense to negate unwanted messages from people, media and unexpected events. Soon, your affirmations will be a part of your life. Writing and reciting will consciously commit them to memory, your subconscious mind will act on them as your beliefs and life will move in your chosen direction, magically.

Affirmation Tips

- Until memorized, read and rewrite affirmations, first thing in the morning.
- Write all affirmations on one 3"x 5" card that you can study regularly. Small print works.
- Always affirm, by repeating three times with enthusiasm, desire and emotion.
- When in the company of others, think through your affirmation, as needed.
- After memorized, choose a time of day that works best for you to state each three times.
- Recall from memory and state at anytime.

Six Steps to Living On Purpose

This page is intentionally blank

Change takes place when we are ready or must. Frequently, it comes at the hands of some trauma in our lives though we have the power to initiate change with sheer will. Regardless of being shocked or willfully moved into changing our lives, we can create the change we desire!

They say you should never volunteer for anything in the military, but when the Commander asked who wanted to deploy early to Iceland, I stood up to be counted—I had a secret. Lucky me, I would be there three weeks before the rest of the boys—plenty of time to stake my claim.

We were the first plane and crew to reach Iceland and the plane's captain took us on a 'fly around' of the island. From my flight station, I gazed out to see nothing but volcanic rock and shouted, "Hey, where are the trees?" All 17 guys on the plane started laughing but me.

"Don't tell me you believed that crap about there being a woman behind every tree?"

Ten weeks later, without the influence of the feminine, without the touch of a woman, there was rustling in the hallway of our condominium-like quarters. I opened my door and was snatched into the long corridor by one of 20 or so brawling fools. I was thrown, tackled and punched before I realized I'd better defend myself in this hallway mayhem. Doors opened from every room and more people piled into the brawl. Serious injury was never the intent and only a few stayed out of the fray.

Not until later, while my roommate and I compared our wounds, did I realized this brawl had occurred out of sheer need for human touch. No women, no touch for many of us! We'd been without human touch for so long, our group consciousness brought it out in the only acceptable form we knew—a big brawl. The innocent brawl had served a real purpose to fulfill the very human need for touch.

Extra Steps:
Engaging Other Senses and Modalities

This section is not a requirement of your program but can aid and expedite your transformation. You have already designed your program for your personal transformation that will bring you the results you desire.

I spent nine months researching, listening to audio programs, watching videos and reading books before I realized I had transformed my life. My primary focus had been listening to positive inspirational speakers and the self-hypnosis/subliminal suggestion tracks. There was relatively no information available on how to use the taste, touch and smell senses to affect my change. So, as a result, I did not pursue the use of these senses consciously. However, there is little, if any doubt, that all the senses or inputs to the brain can play a role in affecting change. Since that time, I have come to understand that *change begets change* or, in other words, making any change in your life makes it easier for more change to occur.

My initial program used only visual and aural stimuli. I did not employ these tools during my transformation, but I feel strongly about their ability to effect change. I have since then experienced these therapies independently and urge you to take advantage of their known benefits. No need to spend extra money here, just consider them as additional tools to aid in your transition should you feel inclined:

1) **Touch** can stimulate change through massage, healing touch, Reiki and even contact sports. Medical facilities worldwide are adding these alternative treatments for a variety of patients. The most popular touch practices include:

   a. **Healing touch**. Using a gentle touch, practitioners use their hands to affect the body's energy fields. Studies show that patients have shorter hospital stays and premature babies grow faster with healing touch.

   b. **Reiki**. This old Tibetan practice, rediscovered by Japanese, allows energy to pass through the hands of the practitioner, who uses a light touch over different parts of the patients body systematically. Studies of patients who have undergone Reiki have indicated they were more relaxed and cooperative before and during surgical procedures.

c. **Massage therapy**. A variety of massage techniques are used to manipulate the body's soft tissues through pressure and movement. Studies have found that systolic blood pressure drops significantly in individuals who receive massage therapy compared with those who do not.

There is a human need for touch and if you aren't getting your share of touch, these are great ways to feel human again.

2) **Tasting** new foods & drinks is a change, and change begets change! The leaders in naturopathic and homeopathic medicine, followed by many allopathic practitioners now overwhelmingly state that the pathological problems westerners have today are a direct result of poor diets and bad eating habits. Western society has moved towards convenience and lost sight of what makes for good diets. Suffice to say, this is a great time to review and change your diet.

There is an abundance of new food information that can be confusing until you get down to the basics—eat real food for a start. Real food consists of fresh fruits and vegetables which also means eliminating processed foods and chemicals appearing as food. Avoid microwave foods that can turn real food into a molecular structure that the body cannot handle and can treat as fat but without the ability to burn it internally. Eliminating most canned food, fast food and eliminating or reducing meats and chemically treated real food is a leap in the right direction to a healthier lifestyle. A healthy diet will have an overall positive effect on your life and move your transformation along.

3) **Aromatherapy** is the use of essential oils, incense and other aromatic compounds, as an alternative physical and mental, to alter moods, mental processes and health. Remember, change begets change, so try smelling something different with the help of a trained aroma therapist. Ever wonder about the effects aromatic and pungent flower leis have had on Hawaiians and their visitors - there is little doubt, aloha spirit has some roots in aromas!

4) Counseling is talking with a *professional without an agenda.* Counseling is a valuable tool in finding alternatives to today's challenges and to expedite transformation. As well intended as family and friends can be, we all have some level of personal agendas. Counselors are trained and practiced at being objective and will guide you to your own solutions.

5) Group therapy offers the rare opportunity to explore and understand interpersonal problems that often stem from our relationships or personal patterns of relating. In group therapy, you can learn and build new relationship skills in an environment of trust and safety. Group therapy is also beneficial to individuals struggling with issues of depression, anxiety, alcohol & drug abuse, medical illness, shyness, loss and a host of other issues. Counseling is for people serious about learning more about themselves and techniques to transform their lives.

6) Physical activity, in addition to getting some exercise, can provide much needed **exposure** to unfamiliar spaces, provoking thoughts of a different kind. When was the last time you walked through a zoo, rowed a boat, hiked in the woods or climbed up a mountain slope? Your TV is turned off and you are not reading a newspaper or glued to a computer screen so now you have time to go try something different. Rather than mindlessly drifting while driving home from work, try taking a different route home or don't go directly home. Make a little change daily!

7) **Make** and **break habits** in 21 days - experience has shown that habits can be created or broken in 21 days. Just think, you can actually start a habit by pushing yourself through 21 days of going to the gym, not smoking or working on your passion. Now is the time to make and break habits, with this secret in hand. If you really want to start working out and don't have the energy, just go to the gym for a few minutes, maybe do one thing but go every day for 3 weeks and you will have established a new habit. Once habitual, you will start working out more passionately. Some habits, like smoking, may require additional support or alternative support, if you have tried and failed. I tried a few "proven" things and failed in attempts to quit smoking. It was not until I picked up a book that explained smoking addiction that I was able to

quit for good without looking back. I imagine the book, *The Easy Way to Quit Smoking,* can be used for many addictions because it commits or convinces your head to quit before approaching the physical aspects of addiction.

8) **Brainwave training** is a technology designed to minimize or eliminate the auto responses attributed to trauma. Some leading neurologists believe that <u>all</u> pathologies, which are any deviations from a healthy, normal, or efficient condition, are the result of major and minor traumas. Brainwave training is designed to clear your mind of the negative auto-responses and open up new pathways for expansion.

One of my favorite things to do when I think I am getting too complacent, is to find something to take me out of my comfort zone. Just to promote and influence growth, I will opt to do something or go somewhere that I am normally resistant to because of my comfort level—big events with large crowds, night clubs, big cities come to mind for me. I am often surprised how much I enjoy such experiences afterwards.

This section should arouse ideas on how you can promote change outside of your six steps and how doing anything different contributes to your transformation. There is no need to tackle this area with any kind of necessity but if the opportunity presents itself to explore something new, why not expedite your change by working outside of your box!

We may not know the limits of our ability to manifest our wants, but there is no doubt that our power is bound by our beliefs of today.

Final Thoughts

Making the choice to transform our lives is to take responsibility for our lives. Our varying beliefs of a higher power is not essential to this decision as we need not relieve ourselves of such beliefs. However, if we deprive ourselves of our free will because of our beliefs, then it would only be appropriate to examine our beliefs and how we have come to possess them. To accept anything that has come to us blindly without critical review, that limits us in any way, should be questioned regardless of how well intended.

When we take back what is rightfully ours and remain vigilant in exercising whatever control we have, we consciously determine how limited and unlimited we are by the beliefs to which we subscribe. Who can say what we are capable of in this life, what are our limits as human beings? We have witnessed others trample boundaries and leap over limitations. So, on the eve of unleashing our own capabilities, leaving mediocrity behind us, where will we go, what will we become of us how will we benefit humanity?

L. Leonard Taylor

References

Abell, Ellen. Too Much TV Can Have Negative Impact on Children. Alabama Cooperative Extension. http://www.aces.edu/dept/extcomm/newspaper/april19d01.html

Allen, James. As a Man Thinketh. London: Allen, 1903.

Apple, Inc. Dictionary. Cupertino: Apple, 2005.

Arntz, Chasse & Vincente. What the Bleep Do We Know? Deerfield Beach: Health, 2007.

Behavior: Secret Voices. Time Magazine. 10 September 1979.

BrainyQuote.com: Gandhi, Mahatma. Hamid, Moshin. Oprah. Plato. Rumi. Streep, Meryl. Internet. www.brainyquote.com, 2001-2014. Electronic.

Brown, Les. Live Your Dreams. New York: Harper, 1992.

Byrne, Rhonda. The Secret. New York: Atria, 2006.

Chapman, Gary. Five Languages of Love. Chicago: Northfield, 1992.

Covey, Stephen. Seven Habits of Highly Effective People. New York: Free Press, 1989

Craigslist. Craigslist Classifieds. San Francisco: http://www.craigslist.org

Demonti, Arrella. The Benefits of Counseling. Internet: RMH Counseling Company. http://www.worldwidehealth.com/health-article-The-Benefits-of-Counseling.html

Diamond, Jared. *Collapse: How Societies Choose to Fail or Succeed. New York: Penguin Group, 2005. Print.*

Donohue, Gene. Creating S.M.A.R.T. Goals. Internet: Top Achievement, http://topachievement.com/smart.html,1998.

Dyer, Wayne. Pulling Your Own Strings. New York: Harper, 1999.

Ehrlich, Steven. Aromatherapy. University of Maryland Medical Center. 7 September 2009. http://www.umm.edu/altmed/articles/aromatherapy-000347.htm

References

Fabricius, David W.A. Vital Seven. Internet webinar. August 2013.

Exercise is the Key to Brain Health Says Study. Huffington Post. 20 September 2011. http://www.huffingtonpost.com/2011/07/21/exercise-brain-health_n_906157.html

Gerdes, Lee. See How Brain State Technologies Can Help. Internet: http://www.brainstatetech.com/how-we-help/process#

Google Search. Finding Your Passion. http://zenhabits.net/the-short-but-powerful-guide-to-finding-your-passion/, http://michaelhyatt.com/find-your-passion-in-three-steps.html, http://www.dumblittleman.com/2010/04/how-to-find-your-passion.html and http://www.ineedmotivation.com/blog/2008/04/7-questions-to-finding-your-true-passion/. Google. Google Website. Mountain View: Google, 1998. https://www.google.com

Graham C.L. Davey, Ph.D. The Psychological Effects of TV News. http://www.psychologytoday.com/

blog/why-we-worry/201206/the-psychological-
effects-tv-news. June 19, 2012

Healing Health Therapies: Alternative Therapies Relax
Heart Patients. Harvard Health. http://
www.health.harvard.edu/press_releases/
healing_touch_therapy. October 2005.

Isaiah 43.7. The Holy Bible.

Jung, Carl G. *The Archetypes and The Collective
Unconscious (Collected Works of C.G. Jung Vol.
9 Part 1)*. New York: Princeton Press, 1969.
Print.

Kenny, Charles. *Americans! Stop Worrying and Learn
to Love Decline: Why 2014 will be our best year
yet.* Internet: POLITICO, January 07, 2014.
Electronic. http://www.politico.com/magazine/
story/2014/01/decline-is-good-for-
america-101749.html#ixzz30bibCxcX

References

Konicov, Barrie. Potentials Unlimited. Internet: Potentials Unlimited, http://potentialsunlimited.com/, circa 1989.

Layton, Julia. Is it True that If You Do Anything for 3 Weeks It Will Become a Habit? Internet: TLC. http://tlc.howstuffworks.com/family/form-a-habit1.htm

ManKind Project. New Warrior Training Adventure. Camp Keanae. Sept. 28, 2013

Matze, Claire. The Incredible Benefits of Touch. BabyZone. http://www.babyzone.com/baby/nurturing/crying/article/benefits-of-touch

Merriman-Webster. Autosuggestion. Internet: http://www.merriam-webster.com/dictionary/autosuggestion

Moore, Robert. *King, Warrior, Magician, Lover: Rediscovering the Archetypes of the Mature Masculine.* New York: HarperCollins, 1990. Print.

Ollman, Bertell. *Market Economy: Advantages and Disadvantages.* Talk at Nanjing Normal University, Nanjing, China. Oct., 1999

Radowitz, John von. Climate change timeline is shocking – scientists. TimesofMatla.com. Electronic. http://www.timesofmalta.com/ articles/view/20131011/environment/Climate-change-timeline-is-shocking-scientists.489854. October 11, 2013.

Robbins, Tony. Awaken the Giant Within. New York: Free Press, 1991.

Ruiz, Miguel. Four Agreements. San Rafael: AmberAllen, 1997.

Sasson, Remez. Power of Affirmations. Internet: http:// www.successconsciousness.com/ index_00000a.htm

Scaer, Robert. *The Trauma Spectrum: Hidden Wounds and Human Resiliency.* New York: W.W. Norton & Company, 2005. Print.

References

Shim, Young Soo. The Impact of the Internet on Teenagers' Face-to-Face Communication. Calument: Purdue University. Volume 6, Issue 10 Spring 2007. http://lass.calumet.purdue.edu/cca/gmj/sp07/graduate/gmj-sp07-grad-shim.htm

Taylor, Charles. Garbage in Garbage Out (Quote). Detroit: Taylor, c1960.

Taylor, Lawrence Leonard. *Six Steps to Transformation.* Lahaina: New World Publishing and Promotions, 2012. Electronic and Print Books.

UC Santa Barbara. Retrieved 2012-11-09. Voter Turnout in Presidential Elections: 1828 - 2008. The American Presidency Project.

Waitley, Denis. Seeds of Greatness. New York: Pocket, 1983.

Wilson, Edward Osborne. *Evolution and Purpose of Man*, interview. Arlington: Public Broadcasting Corporation. Charlie Rose Program. April 5, 2014. Television.

World Factbook 2013-14. Washington, DC: Central
    Intelligence Agency, 2013.

YouTube. YouTube Website. San Bruno: YouTube,
    2005.

Zigler, Zig. See You at the Top. Gretna: Pelican, 1977.

Recommendations

This list of recommended books, videos and audio programs are in alphabetical order by program name. Please check the "Bibliography" if searching by author's name for programs. Many of these programs come in a variety of formats - book, video and audio. I recommend viewing all videos found here and suggest use of audio over book formats because of the ease of use. Audio, of course, can be listened to while driving, walking and performing other tasks where books cannot be consumed. You'll get more program time with audio. Don't forget, listen repeatedly and often for best results and expediting your program.

Please note: At the end of each recommendation there will be an annotation indicating the product's format availability: "V" for video, "A" for audio and/or a "B" for book.

As a Man Thinketh. Allen, James. London: Allen, 1903. http://www.asamanthinketh.net/. B.

Awaken the Giant Within. Robbins, Anthony. New York: Free Press, 1991. A, B.

Recommendations

The Biology of Belief. Lipton, Bruce. New York: Hay House, 2005. B.

The Easy Way to Quit Smoking. Carr, Allen. London, England: Penguin, 1985. B.

Five Languages of Love. Chapman, Gary. Chicago: Northfield, 1992. A, B.

Four Agreements. Ruiz, Miguel. San Rafael: AmberAllen, 1997. A, B.

How to Get What You Want. Zigler, Zig. c1988. A,B.

Limitless. Directed by Neil Burger. 2010. V.

Live Your Dreams. Brown, Les. New York: Harper, 1992. A, B.

Potentials Unlimited. Self Confidence #05, SCII Baroque Music, SKU115SC. Konicov, Barrie. Internet: Potentials Unlimited, http://potentialsunlimited.com/, circa 1989. A.

Recommendations

Pulling Your Own Strings. Dyer, Wayne. New York: Harper, 1999. A, B.

See You at the Top. Zigler, Zig. Gretna: Pelican, 1977. A, B.

Seeds of Greatness. Waitley, Denis. New York: Pocket, 1983. A, B.

Seven Habits of Highly Effective People. Covey, Stephen. New York: Free Press, 1989. A, B.

The Secret. Byrne, Rhonda. New York: Atria, 2006. V,A,B.

What the Bleep Do We Know? Arntz, Chasse & Vincente. Deerfield Beach: Health, 2007. V, A, B.

About the Author

Lawrence Leonard Taylor was exposed to travel by parents who taught in public schools, and spent free summers towing him and his siblings around the country. Lawrence, left Detroit in the late 70's in search of an identity beyond his city borders. In the U.S. Navy, he became an avid chronicler of his travels to foreign lands in letters to family and friends which drew just enough praise to inspire him to develop his storytelling skills.

Lawrence's first major transformation propelled him, with a growing family, into a telecommunications technology and marketing career, delaying his inevitable commitment to writing and publishing. In 2005, semi-retired after moving to Hawaii, he began searching for a method of transforming his life with writing at the core. In recreating his earlier self-styled transformation, he was able to identify six definite steps in his effective change method.

Lawrence Leonard Taylor

Today, Lawrence is a student of human transformation and a proponent of, finding and living on, purpose. "For me, finding and living with purpose is the personal transformation we all strive to make. When we take back our lives, we make a change, the world opens to us, we connect, move beyond old beliefs and limitations and our world becomes a better place. The old paradigm of taking what we can becomes giving what we can."

Lawrence is a father of three and grandfather to seven. He loves hiking and swimming and travels for the exposure and constant change. Lawrence is captivated with the rapid transformation of people, here and now, and has a passion for developing self-sustaining business opportunities. He believes that love, exposure and an open mind are of greatest value to personal development. Lawrence's declared purpose in life "is to build and broaden bridges over the gaps that separate people," because he strongly believes "anything that promotes the separation of people, is not in the best interest of humanity."

The following pages are for
your personal notes.

Personal Processing Notes

Personal Processing Notes

Personal Processing Notes

Personal Processing Notes

Personal Processing Notes

Personal Processing Notes

Personal Processing Notes

Personal Processing Notes

Personal Processing Notes

Personal Processing Notes

Personal Processing Notes

Personal Processing Notes

Personal Processing Notes

Personal Processing Notes

Personal Processing Notes

Personal Processing Notes

Personal Processing Notes

Personal Processing Notes

Personal Processing Notes

Personal Processing Notes

78, 90, 131 I AM 151 167
167

166 photo

7 12
22 26 31
important
child brain, obviously

Made in the USA
Charleston, SC
30 January 2015